Reprints of Economic Classics

PROFITS, INTEREST
AND INVESTMENT

Also by
FRIEDRICH AUGUST VON HAYEK

Reprints of Economic Classics

MONETARY NATIONALISM AND INTERNATIONAL STABILITY

MONETARY THEORY AND THE TRADE CYCLE

PRICES AND PRODUCTION

COLLECTIVIST ECONOMIC PLANNING. *Critical Studies on the Possibilities of Socialism. Edited, with an Introduction and Concluding Essay, by F. A. Hayek.*

JOHN STUART MILL AND HARRIET TAYLOR. *Their Friendship and Subsequent Marriage.*

ROADS TO FREEDOM. *Essays in Honor of Friedrich A. von Hayek. Edited by Erich Streissler.*

PROFITS, INTEREST AND INVESTMENT

AND OTHER ESSAYS ON THE THEORY OF INDUSTRIAL FLUCTUATIONS

BY

FRIEDRICH A. VON HAYEK

Tooke Professor of Economic Science and Statistics in the University of London

AUGUSTUS M. KELLEY · PUBLISHERS

CLIFTON 1975

First Edition 1939

(London: George Routledge & Sons Ltd.)

Reprinted 1969 & 1975 by

Augustus M. Kelley Publishers

Clifton New Jersey 07012

By Arrangement with ROUTLEDGE AND KEGAN PAUL, LTD.

Library of Congress Cataloged.
The original printing of this title as follows:

Hayek, Friedrich August von, 1899–
    Profits, interest, and investment, and other essays on the
theory of industrial fluctuations, by Friedrich A. von
Hayek. New York, A. M. Kelley [1969]

    viii, 266 p. illus. 20 cm.

    Reprint of the 1939 ed.

1. Business cycles—Addresses, essays, lectures.   I. Title.

HB3711.H365 1969   338.54   76–76355
ISBN 0–678–00794–2   MARC

PRINTED IN THE UNITED STATES OF AMERICA
by SENTRY PRESS, NEW YORK, N. Y. 10013
Bound by A. HOROWITZ & SON, CLIFTON, N. J.

CONTENTS

PREFACE

THE essays collected in this volume are a selection from the various attempts made in the course of the past ten years to improve and develop the outline of a theory of industrial fluctuations contained in two small books on *Monetary Theory and the Trade Cycle* and *Prices and Production*. The first and longest of these essays, which has not previously appeared, may perhaps be regarded as a revised version of the central argument of the latter book, but treated from a different angle and on somewhat different assumptions. The others, which have been published at various dates and in various places, deal with different special aspects of the same problem. I have on the whole refrained from revising these earlier essays, except on some minor points of exposition or by inserting a few additional footnotes. Several essays which might have found a place in this collection I have deliberately omitted for a variety of reasons : some, including my discussion of Mr. Keynes' *Treatise on Money*, because they deal with views no longer held by their author ; others, especially an article on the consumption of capital published in a German periodical, because I now realise that part of its theoretical argument was definitely confused ; and yet others because they have either been incorporated in substance in, or bodily added as an appendix to, the second edition of *Prices and Production* (1935).

The essays reproduced here are arranged in inverse chronological order. It is inevitable with a collection of this kind that at least some of the earlier essays are in certain respects out of date and perhaps a word of apology is needed for reprinting them now. But they contain points which I still feel are of some importance and since I do not yet feel ready to give a systematic exposition of the whole of this complex subject, to place these various attempts side by side within the covers of one volume is the best I can do to do justice to the many aspects of it. The last essay in particular, written fully ten years ago and thus antedating *Prices and Production*, has been added only as an appendix. Although I do not now subscribe to all it contains, it still appears to be read, and as it was in a sense the beginning of a continuous development of thought, it perhaps deserves to be made available in a more convenient form.

For permission to republish the various essay included in this volume I am indebted to The Macmillan Company of New York and the Editors of the *Review of Economic Statistics*, the *Quarterly Journal of Economics*, the *Nationalökonomisk Tidsskrift*, and *Economica*.

F. A. von Hayek.

London School of Economics
 and Political Science.
 May, 1939.

I

PROFITS, INTEREST AND INVESTMENT

1. *Introduction.* In this essay an attempt will be made to restate two crucial points of the explanation of crises and depressions which the author has tried to develop on earlier occasions. In the first part I hope to show why under certain conditions, contrary to a widely held opinion, an increase in the demand for consumers' goods will tend to decrease rather than to increase the demand for investment goods. In the second part it will be shown why these conditions will regularly arise as a consequence of the conditions prevailing at the beginning of a recovery from a depression.

The main point on which this revised version differs from my earlier treatments of the same problem is that I believe now that it is, properly speaking, a rate of profit rather than a rate of interest in the strict sense which is the dominating factor in this connection. In particular it seems that the mechanism through which an increase in the demand for consumers' goods may lower the investment demand-schedule (and consequently employment) involves an increase in a rate of profit which is distinct from, and may move independently of, the money rate of interest, although it is often confused with the latter and indeed performs

many of the functions commonly attributed to it.
It will be argued here that it is this rate of profit
which " orthodox " economists, consciously or uncon-
sciously, often had in mind when they spoke of the
rate of interest equalising saving and investment, or
of the rate of interest depending on the scarcity of real
capital.   It will be argued further that this rate of
profit is in many respects much more effective and
fundamental than the rate of interest.   And while it is
easy to understand why economists who were brought
up to think mainly in " real " terms should refer to this
rate of profit as the rate of interest, there can be no
doubt that this practice has caused a great deal of
confusion and that a more careful separation of the
two concepts is necessary.[1]

A second correction of a similar nature concerns the
inadequate distinction I had formerly drawn between
the movements of money wages and the movement of
real wages.   Although the argument of *Prices and
Production* clearly implied a *fall* of real wages during
the later stages of the boom (as is shown particularly
by the discussion of the increasing " price margins "

---

[1] The classical economists were by no means unaware of the fact
that the relationship between the rate of profit and the rate of
interest properly speaking presented a problem.   One of the earliest
questions proposed for discussion at the Political Economy Club
(by G. W. Norman on February 4th, 1822) was " Is there any
necessary connection between the rate of Profit and the rate of
Interest ? " (*Political Economy Club*, Minutes of Proceedings, etc.,
Vol. VI, 1921, p. 11.)   The confusion only began when economists,
probably because of the special associations attached to the word
profit since Marx, began to shun this term and to use interest
instead.   Although in many connections, particularly when the term
interest is used merely as a generic description of the income from
capital in general, as in the theory of distribution, this use of the
term may do no harm, it is definitely misleading in "dynamic "
analysis.

between the various stages of production), this was obscured by the emphasis on the rise of money wages—which is only a symptom that the fall in real wages is having its effect on the demand for labour. There may, however, also have been some confusion between the different ways in which changes in the prices of raw materials and changes in the rate of wages operate. This point will be separately considered in section 9 below.

Apart from these two corrections the main difference between the present version and the older ones is that I am here trying to show the same tendencies at work under different and, I hope, more realistic assumptions. We shall start here from an initial situation where considerable unemployment of material resources and labour exists, and we shall take account of the existing rigidity of money wages and of the limited mobility of labour. More specifically, we shall assume throughout this essay that there is in the short run practically no mobility of labour between the main industrial groups, that money wages cannot be reduced, that the existing equipment is fairly specific to the purposes for which it was made, and finally, that the money rate of interest is kept constant. Terms like income, profits, wages, yields, etc., will throughout, unless the contrary is expressly indicated, be used to refer to amounts of money (as distinguished from the corresponding " real " magnitudes).

The earlier presentation of essentially the same argument in *Prices and Production* has been frequently criticised for its failure to take account of the existence of unused resources. It still seems to me that to start first from a position of equilibrium was logically the right procedure, and that it is important to be able to show how from such an initial position cyclical fluctuations may be generated. But this ought to be supplemented by an account of how such cyclical fluctuations, once started, tend to become self-generating, so that the economic system may never reach a position which could be described as equilibrium. This I shall try to do here and I hope to show that to introduce these more realistic assumptions strengthens rather than weakens my argument.

In a sense the assumptions made here, and particularly the assumption of complete immobility of the rate of interest and of complete rigidity of money wages maintained through the greater part of this paper, are as artificial as the opposite assumption made on the earlier occasions. And I should like to emphasise at once that this paper does not attempt to give a comprehensive or complete account of the causes of industrial fluctuations. It provides merely another theoretical model which ought to help to elucidate certain essential relationships. In particular I want to warn the reader that I do not mean to assert that the rate of profit actually does play quite the role which it is here assumed to play. What I am concerned with is to show how it would act if the rate of interest failed to act at all. I believe that this throws important light on the function of the rate of interest. But it is vain to ask for empirical confirmation of this particular mechanism. All that is relevant for my purpose is whether under the assumed conditions it would act as I describe it.

To concentrate discussion on matters directly relevant to the main problem I have here in general avoided the special terminology of the " Austrian " theory of capital. Although I still regard this theory as essentially right and even as indispensable for a more detailed analysis, I can see that in the simplified form in which I had to use it in my former book it may be more misleading than helpful.   And a systematic discussion of these problems must be reserved for another occasion.

PART I

2. *The Ricardo Effect.* Since throughout this essay we shall frequently have to make use of a proposition of general character, we shall begin by explaining it in its general form quite apart from its special application to problems of industrial fluctuations. Its substance is contained in the familiar Ricardian proposition that a rise in wages will encourage capitalists to substitute machinery for labour and vice versa.[1] Adapted to our present purpose it can best be restated by means of a schematic example. Assume that the labour used directly or indirectly (in the form of machinery, tools, raw materials, etc.), in the manufacture of any commodity is applied at various dates so that Ricardo's " time which must elapse before the commodity can be brought to the market " is two years, one year, six months, three months, and one month respectively for the various amounts of labour used.[2] Assume further that the rate of interest is 6 per cent and that in the initial position the per annum rate of profit on the capital invested in the various kinds of labour is equal to the rate of interest. Assume then that while wages remain constant the price of the product rises by 2 per cent (which means that real wages fall in proportion). The result of this on the rate of profit earned

[1] *Principles,* Ch. I, Section V, *Works,* Ed. McCulloch, p. 26 f.
[2] These various intervals refer to different amounts of labour used in *one and the same* technical process, not to different processes. A change to more or less " capitalistic " processes would be brought about by changes in the proportions of the amounts of labour invested for the various intervals.

on the various kinds of labour is best shown by a table

	Labour invested for				
	2 years	1 year	6 months	3 months	1 month
Initial *amount* of profit on each turnover in per cent	12	6	3	1½	½
	(all corresponding to 6 per cent per annum)				
Add 2 per cent additional profit on each turnover due to rise of price of product ...	14	8	5	3½	½
	which corresponds to a per annum rate of profit of				
	7	8	10	14	30
	per cent				

The amount of profit earned on the turnover of any amount of labour will be equal to the difference between the wages and the price of the marginal product of that labour. If the price of the product rises this will increase the amount of profit on each turnover in a corresponding proportion irrespective of the length of the period of turnover ; and the *time rate* of profit will be increased accordingly much more for labour invested for short periods than on labour invested for long periods. In the case shown by the table the per annum rate of profit is raised, by a rise in the price of the product of only 2 per cent, from 6 to 7 per cent on the two years' investment and from 6 to 30 per cent on the one month's investment. This will, of course, create a tendency to use proportionately more of the latter kind and less of the former kind of labour, *i.e.*, more labour in the last stages of the process and less in the form of machinery or for other work of preparatory character, till by a fall of the marginal product of the former and a rise of the marginal product of the latter kind of labour the time rates of profit earned on capital invested in each become once more the same. Or in other words : a rise in the price of the product (or a fall in real wages) will lead to the use of relatively less machinery and other capital and of relatively more direct labour in the production of any given quantity of output.[1] In what follows we shall refer to this tendency as the " Ricardo Effect."

---

[1] This proposition can be demonstrated by a slight adaptation of the useful diagram employed by Professor Lange to explain the determination of the rate of interest (" The Place of Interest in the Theory of Production", *Review of Economic Studies*, Vol. III/3, 1936, p. 165). Along the abscissa OP is measured the total quantity of labour used in a particular process of production which, it is assumed, can be distributed in various ways between investment for one year and investment for two years. The amount of labour invested for one year is measured from the right to the left so that the remaining portion of the abscissa measures the amount of labour invested for two years. Any point of the abscissa corresponds therefore to a given distribution of the fixed total of labour between the two kinds of investments. The marginal productivity of labour invested for two years (measured along the ordinate OY and on the assumption that the complementary amount of labour is invested for one year) is then shown by the curve sloping down from the left to the right, while the marginal productivity of the various amounts of labour invested for one year is similarly represented by the curve sloping down from the right to the left. It can now be easily shown that the distribution of labour between

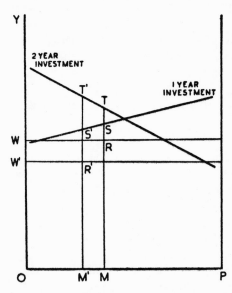

3. *The operation of the " Ricardo Effect " in the later stages of the boom.* We can now apply these considerations to the special case of the rise in prices and fall in real wages which usually occurs in the later stages of the boom. We shall consider an economic system at a point somewhere half-way through a cyclical upswing, when excess stocks of consumers' goods have been absorbed, and employment in the consumers' goods industries is high so that any further rise in demand for consumers' goods will lead to a rise in their prices and a fall in real wages. For the present we shall just take it as a fact—and it is probably one of the best established empirical generalisations about industrial fluctuations—that at this stage prices of consumers' goods do as a rule rise and real wages fall. With the reasons why this should regularly be the case, *i.e.*, why the output of consumers' goods should fail to keep pace with the demand for consumers' goods, we shall be concerned in the second part of this essay. But while in this stage unemployment in the consumers' goods industries will have become insignificant, there may still exist a fairly substantial unemployment in some of the capital goods industries.

the two kinds of investments will be determined by the rate of real wages. Assume wages at first to be equal to OW. Equilibrium requires that the amount of profits on two year investments (neglecting compound interest) be exactly twice the amount of profits on one year investments. These profits are represented by the distances RT and RS respectively and the condition of equilibrium is therefore that $RT = 2RS$. Assume now that real wages are lowered from OW to OW^1. The point at which profits on two year investments R^1T^1 will now be exactly twice the profits on one year investments R^1S^1 will in consequence be shifted to the left, *i.e.*, to M^1. In consequence of the fall in wages the proportional amount of labour used for one year investments will have increased from PM to PM^1, and the corresponding proportional amount of labour invested for two years reduced from OM to OM^1. And the same would apply, of course, to any other pair of investment periods of which the one is longer and the other shorter.

Our next problem is what effect the rise of prices and profits and the fall of real wages in the consumers' goods industries will have on the separate investment demand-schedules (the schedules of the " marginal efficiency of capital ") of the different kinds of capital goods. We shall at first be concerned with the effect of such a rise in prices relatively to cost on the demand for capital goods on the part of the various individual industries, particularly the consumers' goods industries. We shall see later how essential it is, not at once to aggregate the separate investment demand-schedules of the various industries, but carefully to distinguish between the effects which the causes we are considering will have on the demand for different kinds of capital goods. It will be seen then how misleading a premature combination of these separate demand-schedules into one general investment demand-schedule may become in a world where labour (and existing equipment) is not homogeneous, but often very specific to particular purposes, and where, therefore, an increase in the demand for one kind of labour of which there is no more available can in no way offset a decrease in the demand for other kinds of labour of which there is still an unemployed reserve.

Of the three main influences on which the profitability of producing the different kinds of capital goods will depend—their expected yield, their cost of production, and the rate of interest—it will be their yield[1] with

---

[1] It is probably justifiable to assume that expected yields will as a rule move, if not by the same amounts, at least in the same direction as current yields. Whether that is the case or not, however, till it becomes necessary explicitly to bring in expectations, we shall here simply speak of the yield, implying that current and expected yield do move in the same direction.

which we shall here be mainly concerned. It is with
respect to the effect of changes in final demand on the
yield of various types of capital goods that our first
divergence from prevalent views arises ; for it is usually
taken for granted that the yield of capital goods in
general will move parallel with, or at least in the same
direction as, expected final demand.[1]   Now this is true
enough of capital goods (or rather durable consumers'
goods) which without any further collaboration from
labour will directly serve consumption. But it is much
less obvious in the case of labour-saving equipment ;
that is, machinery in the ordinary sense of the word ;
and it is still less obvious in the case of machinery to
make machinery and so forth.

It is here that the " Ricardo Effect" comes into action
and becomes of decisive importance. The rise in the
prices of consumers' goods[2] and the consequent fall
in real wages means a rise in the rate of profit in the
consumers' goods industries, but, as we have seen, a
very different rise in the time rates of profit that can
now be earned on more direct labour and on the

---

[1] This appears to be regarded as so obvious that it is rarely
explicitly stated, except by some general reference to the fact that
the demand for capital goods is " derived " from the demand
for consumers' goods. It is rather instructive that the most elaborate
and influential work dealing with these problems in recent years,
Mr. Keynes' *General Theory*, does not contain, as far as I can see,
any discussion of how a change in final demand affects the yield of
the various types of investment goods.

[2] It should be noted that the relevant rise in the prices of consumers' goods is not the absolute rise, but the rise relatively to
costs of production. This means that an absolute rise in prices
may not have the effects assumed here if it is not in excess of an
independent rise in costs, and that constant prices may have the
same effect as a rise in prices if costs fall (in consequence of improved
technique, previous investments, etc.). The essential point is what
happens to profits.

investment of additional capital in machinery. A much higher rate of profit will now be obtainable on money spent on labour than on money invested in machinery.

The effect of this rise in the rate of profit[1] in the consumers' goods industries will be twofold. On the one hand it will cause a tendency to use more labour with the existing machinery, by working over-time and double shifts, by using outworn and obsolete machinery, etc., etc. On the other hand, in so far as new machinery is being installed, either by way of replacement or in order to increase capacity, this, so long as real wages remain low compared with the marginal productivity of labour, will be of a less expensive, less labour-saving or less durable type.

To illustrate this last point it is convenient to consider for the moment a society where machines are not bought but only hired from the producer. The demand for the services of machines required by the consumers' goods industries, and therefore the rent offered for their hire, will undoubtedly rise in consequence of the increased demand for consumers' goods. But it will not rise to the same extent for different kinds of machinery. A fall in real wages will raise the value of the less labour-saving machinery more than that of more labour-saving machinery, and stimulate the production of the former at the expense

---

[1] Here and throughout the further exposition " the rate of profit " stands for the profit schedule (or the rate of profit on any given output) and the expressions " a rise in profits " and " a fall in profits " must be understood to refer to a rise or fall of the whole profit schedule. On occasions it will also be necessary to speak for the sake of brevity of *the* rate of profit in groups of industries, although this is not intended to suggest that there will be a uniform rise of the profit schedules in these industries. All that is meant is that the rates of profit will tend to rise, to various extents, above the given rate of interest.

of the latter. And similarly with respect to more or less durable machinery. Whether it pays to make machinery more durable will depend on whether the last additional investment by which the life of the machine can be lengthened will bring the same per annum rate of return as the direct use of labour ; and if real wages fall it will evidently be profitable to provide the same services from less durable machinery than before.

4. *The rate of profit and the rate of interest.* The rise of the rate of profit in the consumers' goods industries will then create a tendency for any given quantity of output to be produced with comparatively less capital and comparatively more labour. But, it might be objected, must not the rate of profit always become equal to the rate of interest, which we have assumed to remain constant ? that is, will not production always be expanded to the point where the marginal rate of profit is equal to the rate of interest ? Now this is probably[1] quite true of the *marginal* rate of profit ; but this in no way constitutes an objection to our argument. What we are concerned with are not marginal rates of profit but the rates of profit on any given output and with any given method of production (or the profit schedules or profit curve for all possible outputs and all the various methods of production) ; and the main point is exactly that the only way to make the marginal rate of profit equal to any given rate of

---

[1] At any rate in so far as *expected* marginal profits are concerned. It is, however, by no means unlikely that in the course of such a process of expansion entrepreneurs will find again and again that the prices of their products have unexpectedly risen and that therefore retrospectively marginal profits were persistently higher than the rate of interest.

interest if real wages have fallen is to use a larger proportion of labour and a smaller proportion of capital. If real wages fall and the profit schedule of any given firm is thereby raised, and if the rate of interest remains constant, this will in the first instance mean that more labour will be used with the given machinery till the rate of profit on the marginal unit of labour is once again equal to the given rate of interest. And when it comes to additions to, or replacements of, existing machinery, it will again be the level of the profit schedule and not marginal profits which will determine the kind of machinery that will be installed. Or, to put the same thing differently, a fall in real wages means that the proportion of capital and labour at which the marginal rate of profit on money spent on either will be the same, will be changed in favour of labour, whatever the marginal rate of profit. If, by keeping the rate of interest at the initial low figure, marginal profits are also kept low, this will only have the effect of a reduction in cost, that is, it will raise the figure at which the supply of and the demand for final output will be equal ; but it will not affect the tendency to produce that output with comparatively less capital, a tendency which is caused, not by any change in the rate of interest, but by the shift in the position of the profit schedule.

5. *The role of expectations.* Another possible objection which must be briefly considered here is connected with the expectations of entrepreneurs about future price movements. So far we have considered the effects merely of a single rise in prices of consumers' goods and of the corresponding fall in real wages in the consumers' goods industries ; and the argument

implied that entrepreneurs expect that this higher rate of profit will continue.   But a change in current prices may conceivably affect prices in more than one way and it therefore becomes necessary to consider more explicitly the role played by expectations of the entrepreneurs.   That if entrepreneurs doubt the permanence of the increased demand they will not be inclined to increase the permanent capacity of their plant, and that therefore any idea about a normal price level which is being exceeded will operate in favour of short term rather than long term investment, will probably be granted.   But it might at first appear that if entrepreneurs expected prices to continue to rise indefinitely this would have the contrary effect, that is, would favour investments for long periods. If entrepreneurs did expect a very considerable rise of prices to take place at a fairly distant date, say two years ahead, and if they assumed that prices would then remain high for a fairly long period afterwards, this might indeed stimulate long period investments. But the expected distant rise in prices would have to be very considerable indeed to counterbalance the tendency towards less capitalistic[1] investments caused

---

[1] I am using " capitalistic " and more and less " capitalistic " here very much in the same sense in which Mr. Kaldor in a recent article "Capital Intensity and the Trade Cycle," *Economica*, February, 1939) uses the terms " capital intensity" and " capital intensive " as a somewhat too literal rendering of the German terms " *Kapitalintensität* " *und* " *kapitalintensiv.*"   I have used these German terms myself in the original edition of the " Paradox of Saving."   But the translators (was it Dr. Tugendhat or Mr. Kaldor himself ?) wisely chose to translate them by " roundaboutness " and more and less " capitalistic."   Cf. below, p. 233, footnote.

by a rise in current prices and profits.[1]   If prices, however, are merely expected to continue to rise at the rate at which they have already risen, this will as a rule create the expectation of a continued opportunity to make high profits on short term investments (*i.e.*, it will operate as a rise of the " prices of present goods " relatively to the " prices of future goods " of pure theory), and since the faster prices rise the greater the profit on current turnover is likely to be, the expectation of a continued rise of prices (unless it is an expectation of a rise at a continuously accelerating rate) will operate in favour of short term and against long term investments in the same way as a mere rise in present prices.

6. *The two factors in the operation of the acceleration principle.* The significance of the results so far obtained can perhaps be made clearer if we relate them to a well-known doctrine, the so-called " acceleration principle of derived demand." This doctrine, into the long history and the detail of which we need not enter here, essentially asserts that, since the production of any given amount of final output usually requires an

[1] A reference to the numerical example used before in the text will easily show this. The point is that the expected rise in prices (as a rate per annum) will have to be greater than the rise in the (per annum) rate of profits on current transactions which depends, not simply on the rate at which prices have already risen, but on the ratio of the difference between cost and prices caused by this rise to the period of turnover. If we take the figures used before, where the rise of current profits by 2 per cent (which may be due to a rise of prices extending over the course of some months) has increased the amount of profit on one month's investments from ½ to 2½ per cent, it would require the expectation of a further rise of prices of no less than 46 per cent over the next two years in order to make a two years' investment and a one month's investment equally attractive as they were before. And a still greater expected rise in prices would be necessary in order that long period investments should actually be stimulated.

amount of capital several times larger than the output produced with it during any short period (say a year), any increase in final demand will give rise to an additional demand for capital goods several times larger than that new final demand. The demand for capital goods according to this theory is the result of final demand multiplied by a given coefficient. We shall refer here to the two factors which determine this product as the " multiplicand " and the " multiplier " respectively, the former being final demand and the latter the ratio at which this final demand is transformed into demand for capital goods. (This " multiplier " with which the acceleration principle operates must, of course, not be confused with *the* Multiplier which plays such an important role in Mr. Keynes' theories. We shall later—in section 14 below— have occasion to reintroduce this " multiplier " of the acceleration principle in its inverse form under the name of the " Quotient.")

The characteristic feature of the doctrine of the acceleration principle in its widely current form is that this " multiplier " with which the acceleration effect operates is assumed to be constant—presumably because it is supposed to be determined solely by technological rather than by economic factors. In consequence any change in the " multiplicand "— final demand—is assumed to lead to proportionally a much greater change in the same direction in the demand for capital goods. We have seen, however, that under certain conditions an increase in final demand may lead to a decrease of the " multiplier " ; the provision for supplying the increased demand may be made by using less capital than before per unit of expected demand. And this change will affect not only new investment but equally current replacement demand.

Even if the " multiplier " decreases, however, this does not yet necessarily mean that total demand for machinery and other capital goods on the part of the consumers' goods industries will decrease. Whether this will be the case or not will evidently depend on whether the " multiplicand," final demand, grows more or less rapidly than the " multiplier " decreases. The effect on the demand for machinery of a tendency to increase capacity for final output may or may not be compensated by the tendency to use less expensive kinds of machinery. The net effect will depend on a number of circumstances : the magnitude of the rise in final demand, the durability of the machinery used in the past, the relative magnitude of the demand for additional machinery and of replacement demand (which depends on the two former factors) and finally, on the magnitude of the rise in the rate of profits. It is quite likely, at least as long as the rise of profits is confined to the consumers' goods industries, that aggregate demand for machinery will increase— although it will be demand for different kinds of machinery.

But this is not yet the end of the story. We have so far only considered the situation in the industries serving the consumers directly. We must now subject the situation in the other industries to a similar analysis.

7. *The structure of capitalistic production.* If the idea of a fairly homogeneous aggregate demand for capital goods, more or less directly derived from the

demand for consumers' goods, were an adequate description of reality, little more would have to be said about the subject.   An increase in the demand for consumers' goods that would lead to a decrease in the demand for capital goods, because the increase in the "multiplicand" would be counterbalanced by a decrease in the "multiplier" of the acceleration principle, would be just a theoretical possibility, rather unlikely to occur in real life. Although an increase in final demand would cause changes in the kinds of capital goods demanded, the capital good industry regarded as a unit would almost certainly experience an increase of employment.

But the crude dichotomy of industry into consumers' goods industries and capital good industries is certainly wholly insufficient to reproduce the essential features of the complicated interdependency between the various industries in actual life.   There is every reason to believe that there are as great differences between the position of the different kinds of capital good industries as there are between them and the consumers' goods industries.   The capital goods industries are not all equally adapted to supply the consumers' goods industries with any kind of equipment they may need ; they are further organised in a sort of vertical hierarchy. This fact is essential for our further argument.

Even the concept of the " stages of production " which was intended to supply in the place of the crude dichotomy a somewhat finer distinction is not quite adequate for the purpose.   While this schematic representation brings out one essential fact, the importance of the specificity of existing equipment to a particular method of production, it gives the impression of a simple linearity of the dependency of the various stages of production which does not apply in a world where durable goods are the most important form of capital.[1]

Although it is useful to retain the concept of stages, it is necessary to substitute for our present purpose a somewhat more elaborate pattern for the simple linear arrangement. If we designate the production of consumers' goods as stage I we can then classify the various industries which directly supply the consumers' goods industries with capital goods of various kinds as stages II, III, IV, etc., according to the more or less " capitalistic " character of the equipment which they supply. Stage II would supply the consumers' goods industries with the least capitalistic type of requirements, such as the raw materials and their simplest tools. Stage III would supply them with equipment of little durability and machinery of the least automatic type. Stage IV would supply a somewhat more capitalistic (more durable or more labour-saving) type of machinery, and so on to stage V, VI, etc., in ascending order.

Stage II in turn would obtain its requirements from the higher or earlier stages, i.e., III, IV, V, etc., and distribute its demand between them according to the rate of profit ruling in stage II, and similarly for stage IV, V, etc. It is evident that even this scheme, like every schematic representation, does some violence to reality. In particular, it still gives an undue impression of linearity of these relationships while in fact they may in many respects be rather circular in

[1] In *Prices and Production*, where I used the simple linear stage pattern, the argument was based on the assumption that all capital used was of the nature of circulating capital.

character.[1] But I think that it does at least to some extent reproduce essential features of the real organisation of industry. It shows that while some industries will be more or less directly and predominantly dependent on the demand for capital goods by the consumers' goods industries, others will be designed mainly to serve other capital good industries, and still others will be suited almost exclusively to assist all other industries in the transition to more capitalistic, more labour-saving methods of production.

The further argument turns largely, it will be seen, on the specificity of large parts of industry to comparatively " early " stages of production. But while it is, of course, a question of fact whether this condition is fulfilled in real life or not, and while there may be no single industry whose equipment is so completely specific to the production of particular kinds of capital goods that it can be used only for that and for no other purpose, nevertheless there is no doubt that many industries are largely " specific to the early stages " in the sense that a large part of the output which they are capable of producing can be used only in that very indirect manner. That railroads and shipbuilding and a large section of the engineering industries depend to a great extent on the demand from other industries making capital goods, and that the iron and steel industry in turn is still a stage further removed from consumption (though perhaps to a smaller extent now than before the rise of the motor-car industry) is

[1] Cf. F. Burchardt, " Die Schemata des stationären Kreislaufes bei Böhm-Bawerk und Marx," *Weltwirtschaftliches Archiv*, Vol. 35, No. 1, January, 1932, which, although I cannot agree with all of it, still appears to me not only as the first but also as the most fruitful of all the recent criticisms of the " Austrian " theory of capital.

probably beyond doubt. And there can also be little question that in a modern advancing society there are many specialised plants whose labour and equipment are adapted to provide all the other industries with labour-saving devices of one sort or another which it will be profitable to introduce only if the rate of profit earned with the older methods has fallen to a certain level. In a modern community, particularly after it has gone through a period of low profits and interest rates, quite a considerable proportion of its labour and equipment will be dependent for its employment on a continued transition to (or at least a continued use of) highly capitalistic methods by other industries. The employment of those sections of industry will therefore depend at least as much on *how* the current output of consumers' goods is produced as on *how much* is produced.

8. *The effect on the demand for different kinds of capital goods.* With the help of this schematic representation of the interrelation between the various groups of industries we are now in a position to resume the main argument and to follow somewhat further the effects of a rise in the prices of consumers' goods and of profits in the consumers' goods industries. The first effect, as we have seen, is that while the total demand for capital goods on the part of the consumers' goods industries may possibly decrease but more likely will increase, this demand will be redistributed so that a greater share of it goes to the " later " stages II, III, IV, etc., and a smaller share to the " earlier " stages VII, VIII, IX, etc. The immediate result would then be that the industries belonging to the stages II, III, IV, etc., would experience an increase in the demand for

their products while the industries belonging to the
"earlier" stages would experience a decrease in demand.
For some time this will probably lead to a further
increase in employment, of incomes, and of the demand
for consumers' goods ; the prices of the latter will rise
further and the whole process will be further stimulated.

But as this process continues those capital good
industries the demand for whose products increases
will gradually get in a position similar to that of the
consumers' goods industries ; that is, the industries
in the stages, II, III, IV, etc., will successively reach
full employment, the prices of their products will rise,
wages will fall relatively to the immediate product of
these industries, and profits will rise ; and in consequence these industries, too, will change to less
capitalistic methods of production and shift their
demand for capital goods from the types produced by
the early stages to the types produced by the later
stages.   The industries corresponding to the early
stages will find that the demand for their products
on the part of more and more of the other industries
will fall off.

It is not difficult to see how, as this process continues,
a division of the industries into two groups will gradually
arise : as profits are raised successively in more and
more industries of the first group, the position of the
industries in the second group, which specialise in the
production of very labour-saving or particularly
durable equipment, etc., will be more and more
adversely affected.   And although for a time the
decline of these industries may not be strong enough
to cause a general decrease in the demand for labour,
the point will come when such a decline will set in ;

because, even if aggregate demand for labour at the existing wage level (if to express it as an aggregate has any meaning under the circumstances) continues to increase, it will be an increase in the demand for kinds of labour of which no more is available, while at the same time the demand for other kinds of labour will fall and total employment will consequently decrease.

While, so long as the decrease of the " multiplier " of the acceleration principle through the Ricardo Effect affects only the relation between the last and all the preceding stages of production, it is very unlikely that this decrease will outbalance the increase of the " multiplicand," final demand, the former effect becomes more and more important as it cumulates its effects through successive stages. It is essentially because a large part of final demand has to be transmitted through many successive " stages," in each of which the amount of capital wanted to produce any given output, will depend on the rate of profit earned there, that the magnitude of this " multiplier " with which demand is transmitted becomes of decisive importance. And while at first, when profits have risen only in the consumers' goods industries and the " multiplier " continues to operate with unabated intensity in the earlier stages, the total demand for capital goods will be little affected, yet gradually, as in more and more of the links of the long chain of stages through which demand must pass the ratio of transmission to earlier stages is reduced, the quantitative effects of the reduction in this ratio or multiplier must become greater and greater.[1]

[1] Perhaps this point might usefully be illustrated by a simple diagram similar to those which I have used in this connection on

If the rate of interest had been allowed to rise with the rate of profit in the prosperous industries, the other industries would have been forced to curtail the scale of production to a level at which their profits correspond to the higher rate of interest. This would have

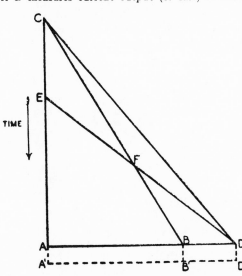

earlier occasions. If in the rectangular triangle $A B C$ the base $A B$ measures current output (or sale) of consumers' goods (as a time rate at a moment), $C A$ the maximum investment period of any of the factors used in the production of this output, the various shorter vertical distances between the line $C B$ and the base $A B$ the corresponding investment periods for the factors used in the further course of the process of production, the area of the triangle will (if for the purpose we disregard interest or profits) represent the magnitude of the stock of capital used in the production of the output. On the assumption that these various investment periods are spread evenly over the total length of the process (represented in the diagram by $C B$ being a straight line), the proportion between the stock of capital and the output of any given period (say the output produced during an interval of the length $A A^1$, represented by the rectangle $A A^1 B^1 B$) will be uniquely determined by the length of the maximum investment period $C A$. This proportion is the same thing as the "multiplier" of the acceleration principle.

Assume now that final demand increases from $A B$ to $A D$. If the "multiplier" remains constant and the additional output is produced with the same amount of capital per unit of output, additional capital goods of an amount corresponding to the area brought the process of expansion to an end before the rate of profit in the prosperous industries would have risen too far, and the necessity of a later violent curtailment of production in the early stages would have been avoided. But if, as we assume here, the rate of interest is kept at its initial level and incomes and the demand for consumers' goods continue therefore to grow for some time after profits have begun to rise, the forces making for a rise of profits in one group of industries and for a fall in the demand for the products of another group of industries will become stronger and stronger. The only thing which can bring this

of $B\ D\ C$ will have to be produced, where the proportion of this quantity to the additional output produced during the unit period $A\ A^1$ will, of course, be the same as that between $A\ B\ D$ and $A\ A^1B^1B$. If, however, as a consequence of a rise in profits the " multiplier " is reduced, the increased final demand will give rise to a demand for capital goods which can be represented by some new triangle of smaller height, such as $A\ D\ E$. It is evident that if as a consequence of a rise in profits the maximum investment period is sufficiently reduced, the total new demand for capital goods represented by the area of ADE may be smaller than the original demand for capital shown by $A\ B\ C$ (which was associated with a smaller final demand). But whether this is or is not the case is not so important as the fact that the demand for resources which are specific to the early stages (here those situated between C and E) will cease and unemployment will ensue here, while the increased demand in the later stages must exhaust itself in a rise in money wages in these stages without creating additional employment.

(Since the diagram shows only " complete" structures in which there is no net investment and therefore total incomes equal to the receipts from the sale of consumers' goods, it does not show why in consequence of the cessation of investment in the early stages total money incomes should fall. But if it is remembered that so long as there is net investment total incomes will be larger than the receipts from the sale of consumers' goods, it will be clear why a reduction of employment in the investment goods industries will lead to a fall in total money incomes.)

The diagram can also be used to illustrate the case where the " multiplier " is reduced in the later stages only but continues to operate with its original intensity in the earlier stages. Such a situation could be schematically represented if in the place of the straight lines $D\ E$ or $D\ C$ we use a broken line such as $D\ F\ C$.

process to an end will be a fall in employment in the second group of industries, preventing a further rise or causing an actual decline of incomes. And if labour is not mobile between the two groups of industries a sort of equilibrium might ultimately be reached with a high rate of profit in the first group and no profits (or profits below the rate of interest) in the second group.

In fact, however, long before this position will be reached, in which there would be only on the one side a group of industries where the rate of profits had risen and on the other a group where yields had fallen, and when there will still be a large intermediate group where neither will have taken place, another adverse effect on profits in the investment goods industries will make itself felt, namely, a rise in costs.

9. *The role of raw material prices.* Up to this point nothing has yet been said on the complicated problem of the rise in costs and particularly of the rise in the prices of raw material on the profitability of the capital good industries. The undoubted fact here is that during the upswing of the cycle raw material prices rise more than the prices of consumers' goods. If this must be regarded as an adverse influence on investment it leads to the apparent paradox that a rise in the " real " value of raw materials (*i.e.*, their value in terms of consumers' goods) has exactly the opposite effect on investment to that of a rise in real wages. The solution of this paradox lies in the fact that while labour, so far as provision for an expansion of output is concerned, is to a large extent a possible substitute for machinery, raw materials are required in practically fixed amounts per unit of output of any particular commodity. While, therefore, a rise in the

price of either machinery or labour may increase the demand for the other of these two factors (and a fall in the price of one will decrease the demand for the other), a rise in the price of raw materials will not only decrease the demand for both labour and machinery, but will also discriminate against the latter because it will at the same time raise the cost of machinery. This means that as the demand for machinery falls in terms of consumers' goods and the prices of consumers' goods fall in terms of raw materials, the producers of machinery (even where the demand for their products has not yet been reduced by a fall in real wages) will be caught between falling prices of their products and rising costs, and will have to curtail production. And this applies not only to raw materials proper. The same will be true of the hundred and one small cost items consisting of the prices of goods, some of them manufactured, such as fuels and lubricants, packing material and stationery, etc., etc. The prices of these commodities which, unlike most labour, are not specific to a particular use but can be shifted between industries and stages will for this reason often move differently from, and perhaps even in a direction contrary to, the prices of many of the products made from them.[1] It is these kinds of commodities, including the raw materials, which are capable of being turned rapidly

---

[1] The same may be true of certain kinds of wages in so far as some types of labour are mobile between industries and the rise of money wages in the consumers' goods industries raises wages of some labour also used in the capital good industries. The case of mobility of labour is here, however, deliberately disregarded. The parallelism between the case of raw materials and some kinds of labour together with a certain confusion between the movement of real wages and the movement of money wages, has, however, to some extent misled me in the discussion of these problems in *Prices and Production*.

and therefore at a fairly high rate of profits into consumers' goods, and the consumers' goods themselves, which are the "circulating capital" which is getting scarce and therefore rises in price.[1]

10. *The decline of investment.* We have now concluded the demonstration of our first thesis, namely that an increase in the demand for consumers' goods may lead to a decrease in the demand for capital goods. It will be remembered that our argument referred throughout to a fairly advanced stage of the boom ; and it is, of course, not argued that any rise in the rate of profit will decrease investment, but merely that, once the rate of profit rises in a sufficient number of industries beyond the rate to which the capitalistic structure of industry is adapted (or in the expectation of which much of the new investment has been started) it will have that effect. All that we were concerned to show is that once a certain point is passed, although the decline of investment may be postponed for a long time by keeping the rate of interest low, it is bound to come, and that the further the point is put off, the greater will be the rise in the rate of profit and consequently also the ultimate decline of investment. The rate of profit will in this case rise more and more, the tendency to increase output quickly will become stronger and stronger, and the range of capital goods that it will no longer be profitable to produce will become larger and larger. The "critical point" where the process enters into the unstable phase has not yet been exactly defined ; that will be one of the main

---

[1] It should perhaps be added here that owing to the great fluctuations in raw material prices the Ricardo Effect is likely to be particularly important through its effect on the demand for capital goods on the part of the raw material industries.

tasks of the second part of this essay. But it must be clear already that this "critical point " does not depend on " full employment " in general being reached, but on the capacity to increase the output of consumers' goods as fast as demand increases.

Our main conclusion reached so far is perhaps that the turn of affairs will be brought about in the end by a " scarcity of capital " independently of whether the money rate of interest rises or not. Up to this point the rate of interest has only been mentioned in passing. But while consideration of its real significance will be deferred to the last sections of this essay, certain conclusions concerning the effects of its failure to rise with the rate of profit may conveniently be made explicit at this stage.

If the rate of interest were allowed to rise as profits rise (*i.e.*, if the supply of credit were not elastic), the industries that could not earn profits at this higher rate would have to curtail or stop production, and incomes and the demand for consumers' goods and profits in the consumers' goods industries would cease to rise. In this way the investment for comparatively long periods, for the " sustenance " of which the current supply of consumers' goods is insufficient, would be cut out. If, however, as we have assumed, the rate of interest is kept at the initial low figure (or if it constantly lags behind the movement of the rate of profits) and investments whose yield is not negatively affected continue in spite of the rise in final demand, the rise of profits in the late stages of production and the rise of costs will both come into play and will produce the result which the rate of interest has failed to bring about. The rise of the rate of profit on short as compared with that on long investments will induce entrepreneurs to divert whatever funds they have to invest towards less capitalistic machinery, etc. ; and whatever part of the required reduction in total investment is not brought about by this diversion of investment demand towards less capitalistic type of machinery will in the end be brought about by a rise in the cost of production[1] of investment goods in the early stages.

Keeping the rate of interest low in spite of a rising demand for consumers' goods cannot prevent the rate of profit from rising ; for just as long as the low rate of interest remains effective it will continue, by stimulating investment, further to increase incomes and the demand for consumers' goods ; and so long as investment continues to increase, the discrepancy between prices and costs of consumers' goods must become progressively larger till the rise in the rate of profit becomes strong enough to make the tendency to change to less durable and expensive types of machinery dominant over the tendency to provide capacity for a larger output. Or, in other words, in the end the " acceleration principle of derived demand " becomes inverted into a " deceleration principle "—and the classical maxims that a scarcity of capital means a scarcity of consumers' goods, and that demand for commodities (=consumers' goods) is not demand for labour assert their fundamental truth.

Some remarks should perhaps be added here on another subject which like the rate of interest will be

[1] Including probably a rise of money wages in these stages, which is, however, here excluded by our assumptions.

considered more systematically later : the assumptions which are implied in our analysis with regard to the rate of saving or the " propensity to consume." Prices of consumers' goods will rise and extra profits will be made on their production so long as a larger part of current money incomes than the replacement cost of current output of consumers' goods is spent on this output. This means that so long as an increase in the demand for consumers' goods proceeds from *net* investment,[1] or, in other words, so long as entrepreneurs invest more than *will* be saved out of the incomes thus increased, prices of consumers' goods must rise relatively to costs. We shall see later to what extent a low propensity to consume (or a great willingness to save out of given incomes) may extend the limits within which such an expansion can proceed without an ultimate breakdown. But even at this stage it must be clear that in order to prevent a rise in profits on consumers' goods nearly the whole additional income created by new net investment would have to be saved. And if in the later stages of the boom further increases in net investment lead first to an increase in the rate of profits and through it ultimately to a curtailment of investment activity, this will clearly be because the marginal propensity to consume is too high and not because it is too low. The apparent exhaustion of investment opportunities at the end of the boom will then be due not to the fact that the investment opportunities which have existed before have all been taken up, but to the fact that because of

[1] On the somewhat complicated way in which net income and net investment must be defined in this context see my article on the " Maintenance of Capital," originally published in *Economica*, August, 1935, and now reprinted below, p. 83 *et seq.*

the rise in the rate of profits in certain stages (that is the *increase* in demand) many kinds of investment which were profitable before have ceased to be so.

11. *Depression and revival.* If in the short run labour is, as we have assumed, highly specific to its particular employment, the unemployment caused by the decline in investment activity will disappear only when investment of the kind in question becomes once again profitable—or in the long run when labour has been gradually transferred to other industries. In order that investment of the former kind should be resumed it is necessary that profits in the late stages of production fall to the former level, or in other words, that the difference between real wages and the marginal product of labour in the late stages should be reduced. But it will inevitably take some time for the decrease in incomes earned in the investment goods industries to lead, *via* a fall of prices of consumers' goods, to a rise in real wages, a reduction of profits in the consumers' goods industries, and ultimately to a renewed stimulus to investment.

Prices of consumers' goods are notoriously sticky. At first, when the demand for such goods ceases to increase or even begins to fall, this will check the tendency to increase capacity and thus (by decreasing the " multiplicand " of the acceleration effect without as yet changing the " multiplier ") will decrease employment also in those capital goods industries which till the end shared the prosperity of the consumers' goods industries. This will further intensify the decrease of incomes and of consumers' demand. When the prices of consumers' goods begin at last to fall, this will affect producers of consumers' goods the more the further they have gone in changing to methods with a high proportion of labour costs of production. But gradually, as employment falls in these industries, too, and as the producers with the highest proportion of labour costs are being eliminated, further falls in demand will lead to comparatively smaller reductions of production and employment. It is clear that this process will take longer according as the preceding boom has lasted longer and the tendency towards the adoption of more costly (less capitalistic) methods of currently producing consumers' goods has been carried further. Even if we disregard here completely any monetary complications which may be caused by the shock to confidence, this process of contraction may well last long enough for the volume of employment and of incomes to be considerably reduced. In the end, however, a new position of temporary quasi-equilibrium would be reached in which, with a very low general level of employment, the demand for consumers' goods will once again have become equal to current output, and output and production will cease to shrink further.

At some stage of this process, however—either before this point is reached or soon afterwards—a contrary tendency brought about by the rise in real wages will make itself felt. We find now the obverse of what we have seen to happen during the later stages of the boom. While for a considerable time the factor dominating the demand for investment goods will be the decrease in the capacity needed in the consumers' goods industries (the " multiplicand " of the acceleration effect), a point will come when this tendency will be overcome by the increase of the amount of investment that will be wanted for any given amount of output (*i.e.*, of the " multiplier "). The fall in the rate of profit and the rise in real wages will make a " substitution of machinery for labour " profitable, and although at first the effect of this may be small, a point will be reached when the maintenance even of a small capacity of producing final output, corresponding to the reduced current demand for consumers' goods, by the more efficient, more capitalistic methods corresponding to the higher level of real wages, will lead to an increase of investment.   Although with the given demand it will not be profitable to produce more consumers' goods (*i.e.*, to produce a final output of greater total costs), it may well be profitable to increase investment beyond current amortisation in order to reduce costs of production.   But this in turn will increase incomes and demand and the upward movement will start again.

It is not intended to give here a complete account of all the phases of the cycle and this rapid sketch of the forces operating during the downward swing of business activity must suffice to show that even during this phase it may be not so much the money rate of interest as the rate of profits and real wages which govern the decline and eventual revival of investment. We must, however, give more attention to the early stages of the process of revival. It is here that we shall have to face the crucial question which we have not yet answered, namely why it is that in the course of the recovery the supply of consumers' goods will become insufficient, or where the " critical point " lies beyond which the expansion of investment will create an inherently unstable position. The second part of this essay will be devoted mainly to this problem.

PART II

12. *Factors governing the revival of investment.* We shall assume that general activity has fallen to a very low level before investment and incomes begin to rise again. This means that unemployment will be very high, prices of consumers' goods and profits exceptionally low, and real wages comparatively high. The low rate of profits means here a low rate on working costs, because if all costs were taken into account it may well be that in many cases prices do not even cover replacement costs and that there will be a general under-maintenance of capital.[1] In a sense the low rate

[1] For some curious reason there appears to be less objection to the term under-maintenance of capital than to the term consumption of capital, although the two terms clearly mean the same thing. It is now probably generally admitted that some consumption of capital is a characteristic feature of every major depression (on this see now S. Fabricant, *Capital Consumption and Adjustment*, New York, 1938). But who has ever suggested, as is alleged by Mr. Keynes (*General Theory*, p. 329), that the boom is characterised by capital consumption ? All that could be reasonably said is that towards the end of a boom an increasing tendency towards capital consumption develops which ultimately brings investment to a standstill. But long before there can be any question of net capital consumption the system will have gone far into depression. The opposite type of misunderstanding occurs in a recent article by Mr. N. Kaldor which in certain other respects resembles my present (and earlier) argument. (Cf. "Capital Intensity and the Trade Cycle," *Economica*, February, 1939.) In order to prove that the results of his analysis on the central point are different from those of the "Austrian" theory (which in other respects they certainly are !) he asserts that "the proposition underlying the Austrian theory of the trade cycle—that the boom is characterised by the adoption of

38

of profit and the high real wages may even be regarded as a result of under-maintenance of capital, since the income generated by merely using (but not replacing) existing equipment will be lower than total replacement cost of current output, and the labour employed in producing current output will have to share this output with fewer people engaged in replacing equipment.

With high real wages and a low rate of profit[1] investment will take highly capitalistic forms : entrepreneurs will try to meet the high costs of labour by introducing very labour-saving machinery—the kind of machinery which it will be profitable to use only at a very low rate of profit and interest. The first increase of investment, induced by the high real wages, would not aim at producing a larger final output. It would entirely take the form of what Wicksell called a growth of capital in height and what Dr. Hawtrey has recently

more capitalistic methods of production, and the depression by a return to less capitalistic methods—ought . . . to be reversed." I do not know whether any member of the " Austrian School " has ever used this loose language, but it will be evident from the text that the terms boom and depression are far too vague to describe the real situation. (Is " boom " equivalent to the whole upswing of the cycle and " depression" to the downswing, or the former to the whole upper half and the latter to the whole lower half ?) What I have argued before and is equally implied in all other versions of the Austrian theory of the trade cycle is that the transition to more capitalistic methods of production takes place during periods of low interest rates and *brings about* the boom, and that the transition to less capitalistic methods of production is caused by the high rates of interest and brings about the depression. This is of course very different from what Mr. Kaldor alleges to be the Austrian position and is practically identical with his own " new " theory on this point. The only point on which I now want to modify this earlier statement is the substitution of high and low rates of profit for high and low rates of interest.

[1] Wages, in terms of the immediate products of the industries concerned, will be even higher and the rate of profit even lower in the early stages than in the consumers' goods industries.

called a " deepening " of capital.[1] Or, we might say, it is entirely due to an increase of the " multiplier " of the acceleration principle while the " multiplicand " remains unchanged. The increase of investment outlay beyond current receipts from the sale of final output would therefore also be merely temporary, since once the equipment had been increased to the desired magnitude, replacement demand would again be no larger than receipts from the sale of final products. This at least would be so if the increase of investment did not in turn lead to an increase of incomes and thus to an increase in consumers' demand. But as consumers' demand will increase in consequence of the additional income generated by the new investment, the increase in investment will not only be maintained but will even be stimulated further.

This further increase of investment will mean that capital will now grow in " height " and " width " at the same time, that a process of deepening and a process of widening will proceed simultaneously. Or at any rate, so long as real wages and profits remain at the initial level, the tendency to produce any

[1] Cf. K. Wicksell, *Lectures on Political Economy*, Vol. 1, pp. 163 and 266, and R. G. Hawtrey, *Capital and Employment*, 1937, p. 36. There is a slight difference in the distinctions drawn by the two authors, as Dr. Hawtrey applies his distinction to individual industries while Wicksell applied it to the economic system as a whole. The consequence is that an expansion of the very capitalistic industries at the expense of the less highly capitalistic ones would be treated as a case of mere widening by Dr. Hawtrey while Wicksell would have regarded it as a growth in height of the capital structure of the whole system. Much of what follows is implicit in the point made by Dr. Hawtrey that changes in the rate of interest are associated only with the deepening but not with the widening process—although we should have to substitute rate of profit for rate of interest.

additional output with the use of a high proportion of capital will persist. And as in consequence of this investment final demand increases further, provision has to be made to produce a larger and larger output with these highly capitalistic methods. It is in this phase of the revival, before prices and profits begin to rise, that the acceleration principle operates with a constant (and very high) multiplier, that every (actual or expected) increase in the demand for consumers' goods will lead to a demand for a very great quantity of capital goods and that employment will grow rapidly in the investment goods industries.[1]

There can be little doubt that with much unused equipment in the consumers' goods industries and large surplus stocks in all the late stages of production it will be possible for recovery to proceed a long way before the prices of consumers' goods and profits will rise and real wages fall. And till the (present or expected) rate of profits begin to rise, investment will continue to take the highly capitalistic forms. But as every increase of net investment means that incomes grow more than the output of consumers' goods, it is clear that this process cannot go on indefinitely without causing a rise in prices and profits and thereby adversely affecting the profitability of the more

[1] It should be remembered, however, that the acceleration principle will not begin to operate so long as there are unused resources of *all* kinds available. The relationship between the degree of employment and the operation of the acceleration principle is, however, exceedingly complex and cannot be discussed here. Detailed analysis would show that it can neither operate when there are unused resources of all kinds, nor when there are no unused resources, but only in the intermediate positions which will, of course, be the rule.

capitalistic investment undertaken. What are the limits within which this process of expansion can proceed without causing a rise in prices and profits and thereby making the more capitalistic types of investment less profitable ?

13. *Inflationary and non-inflationary increases of money incomes.* In general terms the answer to our last question is obvious : the demand for consumers' goods arising out of the increased incomes must not increase faster than the supply of consumers' goods will be increased. And for a considerable time after the beginning of the recovery there will be no difficulty about increasing the output of consumers' goods rapidly. As has been mentioned already, the first impact of the increased demand will be met from the stocks accumulated during the depression—the only form in which some of the savings of the past could be stored up. In addition it will be possible, by taking idle equipment into use, to increase the current output of consumers' goods[1] not only quickly but also with an additional disbursement of working costs which will be considerably smaller than the value of the additional

---

[1] As it is sometimes alleged that the " Austrians " were unaware of the fact that the effect of an expansion of credit will be different according as there are unemployed resources available or not, the following passage from Professor Mises' *Geldwertstabilisierung und Konjunkturpolitik* (1928, p. 49) perhaps deserves to be quoted : " Even on an unimpeded market there will be at times certain quantities of unsold commodities which exceed the stocks that would be held under static conditions, of unused productive plant, and of unused workmen. The increased activity will at first bring about a mobilisation of these reserves. Once they have been absorbed the increase of the means of circulation must, however, cause disturbances of a peculiar kind."—In *Prices and Production*, where I started explicitly from an assumed equilibrium position, I had, of course, no occasion to deal with these problems.

output (at current prices)[1] ; in consequence, even if all the new income created in the consumers' goods industries is immediately spent on consumers' goods, there will still be a surplus of output left to meet some part of the demand of those newly employed in the investment goods industries.   Whatever is being saved by those engaged in currently turning out consumers' goods provides a further source from which the demand for consumers' goods on the part of those who produce investment goods can be supplied.   And after a while the activities of the latter will begin to make a contribution to the current flow of investment goods.

But does not the mere fact that money incomes increase throughout this process prove that more is being invested than is being saved (*i.e.*, that money that has not been earned in production becomes available for expenditure on products) ?   And does this not mean that the demand for consumers' goods must rise faster than supply ?   In the conditions which we are considering here the position is not as simple as this.   If we started from a position of full employment the answer to those questions would indeed be " yes."   New investment then would mean that resources are diverted from producing consumers' goods to producing capital goods ; the larger money incomes would meet a decreasing output of consumers' goods ;   and the saving that is required to finance the

---

[1] The reason why this unused equipment was not used although prices would have covered current outlay connected with it (factor cost) is, of course, that before the increase in demand prices obtainable for additional output would not have covered " user cost " in addition to " factor cost."

new investment would in this case have to mean an actual decrease of consumption.

The situation is, however, different when the savings of one group of people are used to maintain formerly unemployed people while they are employed producing investment goods. In this case saving and investment on the part of the first group of people will not lead to a reduction of total consumption but only to a transfer of consuming power to a second group of people.[1] And since there is no reason why total consumption should be decreased in this case, there is also no reason

---

[1] It is in this case, and in this case only that Adam Smith's famous dictum applies that " what is annually saved is as regularly consumed as what is annually spent, and nearly at the same time too ; but it is consumed by a different group of people." (*Wealth of Nations*, Bk. II, Chap. 3, Ed. Cannan, Vol. I, p. 320.) The main idea of this argument has been given wider currency through J. S. Mill's " third fundamental theorem respecting capital," namely that " although saved, and the result of saving, it is nevertheless consumed " ; or, as Mill puts it in another place, when income is saved, the savers " do not thereby annihilate their power of consumption ; they do but transfer it from themselves to the labourers to whom they give employment." (*Principles of Political Economy*, Chap. 1, Sections 5 and 3, Ed. Ashley, pp. 70 and 68.) In an economy with unemployed resources a fuller analysis would have to distinguish between three successive stages in the process of saving and investment : in the first stage it will be possible to invest more and at the same time to increase the output of consumers' goods so as to leave real wages of the increased number employed unchanged ; in the second stage while it will still be possible to invest more without decreasing the output of consumers' goods, but the given (or only slightly enlarged) output of consumers' goods will have to be shared among the larger number of workmen now employed and real wages will fall ; in the third stage a further increase of investment will be possible only at the price of an actual decrease in the output of consumers' goods, because it will involve a diversion of resources from the production of consumers' goods to the production of capital goods. While if we started from a position of equilibrium (as I did in *Prices and Production*), only the third case would be relevant, it is disregarded here because we assume that labour is completely immobile in the short run. It is, however, probably not without importance in some major booms.

why the part of the total money incomes which is available for expenditure on consumers' goods should fall. But this means that total money incomes must increase by exactly the amount by which saving and investment lead to the employment of formerly unemployed resources.

It can be easily shown that unless in this case money incomes were increased to the required extent, saving would have a definitely deflationary effect and, therefore, that an increase of money incomes within these limits would not be inflationary.[1] In the first instance it should be clear that when savings are used to redistribute consuming power so as to give people formerly unemployed a share in the current output of consumers' goods as remuneration for their producing investment goods, this means that the same income, or the titles to the same shares of the current output of consumers' goods, have to be paid out twice over : first to the people who save and invest that income, and then to the people who receive it for making capital goods and who spend it on consumers' goods. If the

[1] The criterion for "inflationary" or "deflationary" seems to me to be as follows. There is neither inflation nor deflation if (1) there occurs no change in prices unless it is necessary for the restoration of equilibrium either that the production of the commodities affected should be increased or reduced, or that the recipient of the income affected should permanently (i.e., till the next real change) get a larger or smaller real income ; and (2) if no price change necessary for this purpose is prevented. All monetary changes which do not fall in this category have the characteristic attribute that their effects are self-reversing, that is that they will cause further price changes which in the end will reverse the real change caused by the impact effect of the monetary change. (On the significance of these " self-reversing changes " see my *Monetary Nationalism and International Stability*, 1937, *passim*.) Applied to the present case this means mainly that unless it is necessary that the output of consumers' goods should be reduced the prices of consumers' goods should not fall relatively to costs.

latter are, however, to step effectively into the gap in the flow of consumers' demand caused by the saving, they will have to be given, in addition to the money saved and invested by the others, and actually before that money reaches them, an amount of money sufficient to build up whatever cash balances they intend to hold when their income will be increased. Only if this is the case will they be able to start buying consumers' goods as soon as the others cease to do so : and only in this case will the money stream continue to reach the consumers' goods market at a constant rate.[1]

So long as the increase of money incomes does not increase the demand for consumers' goods by more than the amount by which, at the time this new demand reaches the market, other people will be willing to increase their saving, total demand for consumers' goods will not increase. The increase of money incomes in this case really means that future savings are anticipated (in the literal sense of the word, *i.e.*, they are not merely foreseen, but the possibilities of increasing investment which are created by the future saving are made use of before these savings are actually made).

But, as we have already seen, it is not merely the

---

[1] Some considerations of this sort were evidently at the basis of the discussion of the " circuit flow of money " in the various works of Messrs. Foster and Catchings. But they neither made it clear that the argument applied only in so far and to the extent that savings were used to employ formerly unemployed factors, nor do they appear to have been aware in what way this innocuous increase in money incomes was limited by the future rate of savings. My criticism of their views expressed in the article on the " Paradox of Saving " reprinted below ought, however, to be supplemented by the considerations developed here.

increase in net savings following the increase in incomes which in the course of the revival will allow an increase of employment in the investment goods industries without this leading to a rise in the prices of consumers' goods and in profits. There is also the increase in the output of consumers' goods in excess of the cost of working existing equipment which can be used to sustain additional people producing capital goods. And as the revival proceeds some of the new investment made in the course of it will begin to contribute to the current flow of consumers' goods. All these sources contribute to the fund out of which the new demand for consumers' goods from those producing investment goods can be satisfied.

We can now make somewhat more precise our former statement about the limits within which the expansion of investment must keep if the rate of profit is not to rise : the increase of money incomes resulting from an increase of investment will not bring about a rise in prices and profits in the consumers' goods industries if by the time part or all of this new income is spent on consumers' goods, either savings, or the value of the output of consumers' goods (in terms of replacement costs), or the sum of these two magnitudes, increase by a total amount equal to that new demand. Is the rate of expansion, once the revival has set in, likely to keep within these limits if the supply of credit is highly elastic and the rate of interest kept at the initial figure ?[1]

---

[1] These considerations also appear to provide the answer to a difficulty which has much puzzled me on earlier occasion, namely the question of what constitutes " neutral money " in a progressive society where the quantity of " original " factors and particularly population increases. The conclusion which then seemed to me to

14. *Different forms of investment distinguished according to the rate at which they will contribute to the flow of consumers' goods.* The answer to the last question depends largely on the form the new investment will take. We have seen before that total investment will be determined as the product of two factors : the volume of investment per unit of expected demand (the " multiplier ")—which varies inversely with the rate of profit—*times* the number of such units which demand is expected to reach (the " multiplicand "). Various combinations of rates of profit and expected volumes of demand may therefore lead to the same amount of investment ; but equal amounts of investment which will generate the same additional money income will therefore differ in one very important respect according as they are the result of a high expected demand *plus* a high rate of profit or the result of a low expected demand *plus* a low rate of profits. If a given amount of investment has been guided by a comparatively low rate of profit, the rate at which this investment will contribute to the output of consumers' goods will be slow ; after investing in that form at a given rate for a period of, say, one year, the rate at which at the end of that year we shall have contributed to the current output of consumers' goods may be only a small fraction of the rate at which we have been investing during the year ; £5,000 invested in the

be inescapable and which I drew reluctantly, that even in this case aggregate money incomes ought to be kept constant (*Prices and Production*, 1st Ed., p. 90, 2nd Ed., p. 107), was therefore erroneous. The cases of an increase of productivity of a given supply of factors and of an increase in the supply of these factors are not, as I then thought, similar but fundamentally different.

course of a year in a very durable building may yield only services of a value of £300 p.a. If the investment had been guided by a higher rate of profit this rate at which a given amount of investment will contribute to the stream of consumers' goods would be higher.

Without entering here deeper than is necessary into the intricacies of the theory of capital it will be useful somewhat further to elaborate this proposition that the lower the rate of profit and the more " capitalistic " therefore the type of investment undertaken, the slower will be the rate at which after any given interval a given expenditure of investment will contribute to the output of consumers' goods. If a building is made more durable, the rate of flow of services from it will, during any given period, bear a smaller proportion to the cost of constructing it than would be the case if it were less durable. If more expensive and more labour-saving machines are introduced in the manufacture of any commodity, the value of the output during any given period will also bear a smaller proportion to the initial expenditure on starting the new process. The same will be true if industries requiring comparatively more capital expand more than others, or if in any other sense more roundabout methods are introduced. It will be convenient to call for our present purpose this proportion of the current contribution to the flow of consumers' goods after, say, one year, to the amount of investment during that year to which it is due, the Quotient or simply Q—although this simple concept would hardly be adequate for any more systematic treatment of the theory of capital.[1] It will at once be obvious that Q is simply the inverse of the " multiplier " of the acceleration principle, so that, if Q is 1/10, a given increase in final demand will tend to increase investment by ten times this amount and so on.

Less obvious but equally important is the fact that Q also tells us how long any new investment at a given rate will have to continue before the resulting addition to the capitalistic structure of production will be " complete " and self-maintaining, *i.e.*, till the mere maintenance of the existing structure without any further net investment will require continued production of capital goods at a constant rate.[2] If, *e.g.*, Q is 1/10 and investment of this kind at a constant rate continues for ten years the contributions to current output of consumers' goods due to this investment will grow year by year from 1/10 to 2/10, 3/10, and so forth, of the amount of annual (gross) investment, and the part of the investment that is net will correspondingly decrease, till in the tenth year the output of consumers' goods will have become equal to current gross investment ; and this latter will have ceased to be net investment in any part, as it will have to continue at a constant rate merely to maintain current final output.

[1] The defects of this concept are essentially the same as those of the concept of the " average period of production " to which it is indeed related in a very simple manner ; like the latter it can be used in most connections only if we assume that the results of the investments made at any moment are spread evenly over a definite period of time ; and it disregards various complications introduced by the rate of interest. But it has probably the advantage over the latter concept of referring to more concrete facts.

[2] See on this point the well-known discussion between Professor R. Frisch and Professor J. M. Clark on " Capital Production and Consumers' Taking " in the *Journal of Political Economy* for 1931 and 1932.

The last point is of special interest to us as it is *net* investment, and net investment only, that creates incomes in excess of the value of the current final output, and in connection with which a problem of the relation between it and (net) saving arises.[1] An increase merely of gross investment without a simultaneous increase in net investment must mean that the output of consumers' goods has increased by the same amount (or merely that some commodities change hands more often than before, which under the " gross " approach would have to be treated as an increase of output). And similarly, an increase merely of gross incomes will as a rule[2] mean that gross saving and gross investment have simultaneously changed by identical amounts. It is only in connection with changes in net investment and consequently of net income that the problem arises whether this will be matched with a corresponding change in net saving, or what the marginal propensity to consume will be.[3]

[1] The definition of net saving and net investment is undeniably difficult, and still more so is the measurement of their magnitude since the distinction must inevitably be based on subjective criteria ; but I cannot see that this is an argument for substituting for these " net " concepts the quite irrelevant " gross " concepts. The mere fact that when one uses the gross concepts the definition of what is and what is not investment is necessarily purely arbitrary and that it does not matter where we draw the line shows that it is an altogether irrelevant, if not meaningless magnitude. That the definition of what is net income, net saving, and net investment must be based on subjective factors these concepts have in common with all other concepts of economic theory. On the whole question see my article on the " Maintenance of Capital " reprinted below.

[2] An exception of considerable importance for trade cycle theory is the treatment of capital gains, particularly of speculative profits on the stock exchange, as net income.

[3] To speak of a given marginal propensity to consume with respect to gross incomes and irrespective of its composition of net income and mere amortisation quotas appears to me an altogether unjustifiable procedure.

While changes merely in gross investment, without a change in net investment, as it were " finance " themselves (because *ex definitione* there must be a corresponding change in the production of consumers' goods or in gross savings), it is only in connection with net investment that the problem arises whether or not they will be equalled by independent decisions to perform net saving.

15. *The demand for, and the supply of, consumers' goods during the upswing.* We have seen that a low rate of profits will tend to make incomes grow relatively fast and the output of consumers' goods grow relatively slowly, while a high rate of profit will tend to make incomes grow relatively slowly and the output of consumers' goods grow relatively fast. And it follows from this that if the initial rate of profit were too low it must lead to an increase in incomes and in the demand for consumers' goods which sooner or later would exceed the supply, and therefore to a rise of profits ; and that if the initial rate of profits were too high it would sooner or later lead to an increase of output in excess of the increase in demand and therefore to a fall in the rate of profit. And there will be one rate at which net investment will grow at the same rate as net saving and the output of consumers' goods will grow so that the rate of profit will remain stable. Is the initial rate likely to be that equilibrium rate, or is it likely to be above or below it ?

The first point to be noted here is that the initial rate of profit will be low, not because the rate of saving at this stage will be high, but because total incomes will be low : the income available for expenditure on consumers' goods will be small compared with their total cost because only part of the equipment used in their production will be currently replaced. But this provides no reason to expect that when incomes grow the part of them which is spent on consumers' goods will grow no faster than the output of consumers' goods. To prevent this it would by no means be sufficient that savings should grow in proportion with incomes[1]; because the proportional share of the total income which is derived from net investment will increase ; and to prevent the rate of profits from rising it would be necessary that total net saving should increase *pari passu* with net investment.

At first, and for some time after the beginning of the revival, the rate at which the output of consumers' goods increases will be comparatively fast, the amount of net investment comparatively small, and Q for the *total* new employment comparatively high : while the new investment will generate much more income than it contributes to the output of consumers' goods, it will be possible, by taking idle machinery in the consumers' goods industries into operation, to add to the current output of consumers' goods while at the same time disbursing less in costs than their current value. But

[1] As it has been seriously suggested that until comparatively recently most economists were unaware of the fact that a rise in incomes will lead to a rise in saving I may perhaps be permitted to refer to the closing sentence of my article on " Saving " in the *Encyclopædia of the Social Sciences* (reprinted, partly for this reason, later in this volume), which treats this fact, in conformity with the views generally held at the time of its publication, as a self-evident commonplace. It was indeed so much taken for granted that in the German discussions of this sort of problem ten years ago the only point at dispute was whether the increase of voluntary savings following a credit expansion would or would not equal the " forced savings " brought about by that expansion.

since the amount of unused capacity in the consumers' goods industries is even in the depth of a depression usually fairly limited, and since the fact that equipment is currently replaced by more capitalistic, more labour-saving, kinds will tend at first to decrease rather than to increase total capacity,[1] this tendency will continue only for a comparatively short period. And as the rate of investment continues to increase the proportion of total income that is earned from net investment will likewise increase, and therefore, if profits on the production of consumers' goods are not to rise, the *proportion* of incomes that is saved will have to increase parallel with the proportion of total income that is earned from net investment. (This will at least be true if, as is likely to be the case, the rate at which investment increases is greater than Q, *i.e.*, greater than the rate at which current investment will contribute to the output of consumers' goods.[2] Or, in other words, if Q is smaller than the marginal propensity to consume, the point is bound to come when the demand for

[1] While this more expensive kind of machinery will, of course, produce more per unit of collaborating labour, it will produce less during any unit of time per unit of its own costs—at any rate if the introduction of the new machinery is not the result of a new invention but of a rise in real wages and a fall in profits. The result of such a conversion of a given amount of existing capital into more " capitalistic " forms will therefore be that it will now be capable of turning out consumers' goods only at a smaller rate than before. (The potential gain consists in that in consequence labour is released for other purposes.)

[2] If the proportion by which investment increases during any given period, say a year, is greater than the proportion by which this investment at the end of this period will have contributed to the output of consumers' goods (*i.e.*, greater than Q), this will necessarily lead to a cumulative increase of net investment. If investment increases at a rate smaller than Q, however, net investment will tend to decrease.

consumers' goods will rise more rapidly than the supply of consumers' goods, and profits in the consumers' goods industries will begin to rise.)

16. *The anomaly of the cumulative process.* The rise of the rate of profit in the consumers' goods industries above the initial low level is probably inevitable if investment revives at all fast. But at first this increase of profits may not matter. Profits may not have been expected to remain at the very low initial level. Since such a rise of profits, even if it only confirms expectations, is, however, likely to stimulate investment further, they will continue to rise, and sooner or later increase beyond the level that was foreseen when investment began to revive.

Even when profits begin to rise beyond expectations this will for a considerable period serve to increase further the total amount of investment. At first the rise in the rate of profit will be confined to the consumers' goods industries. If this led immediately to a similar rise in the rate of interest, marginal rates of profit would everywhere have to be adjusted to this higher rate of interest and activity in the investment good industries would have to be reduced till this was the case. But if the rate of interest does not rise at this stage the increase of profits in the consumers' goods industries will, as we have seen, for some time stimulate investment further (the reduction of the " multiplier " will at first be less effective than the increase of the " multiplicand "). We get then the anomalous position that an increase in the demand for consumers' goods will further increase the proportion (and the absolute amount) of incomes earned from net investment so that the discrepancy between the demand for consumers' goods and the supply of consumers' goods must get larger and larger. It is this anomaly that the increase in the demand for consumers' goods will for some time increase the output of investment goods more than the output of consumers' goods, and that every further increase in investment will increase profits on consumers' goods still further, that makes the position inherently unstable. It is a cumulative process, indeed an explosive process, leading further and further away from an equilibrium position till the stresses become so strong that it collapses.

The popular idea that an increase of investment will necessarily lower the rate of profit to be earned is true only of equilibrium conditions where no more income is derived from investment activity than will be saved. But once investment exceeds the amounts that will be saved out of the income thus increased, this can bring only a further rise and never a fall in profits ; and since, so long as a rise in profits still further stimulates investment, this can only lead to a further gain of investment over saving and a further rise of profits, the process can only come to an end when the rise of profits begins to operate as a curb to investment in the way explained before. Once the cumulative process has been entered upon the end must always come through a rise in profits in the late stages and can never come from a fall in profits or an exhaustion of investment opportunities.[1]

---

[1] An exhaustion of investment opportunities and over-investment in this sense may, of course, occur in particular industries, as for instance in the building or the motor-car industry. It means that most of the additional income generated by the investment in these industries is not spent on the product of these industries but on the products of other industries. In this case, however, while profits fall and investment declines in the industries where the over-investment

17. *The short run ceiling of stable employment.* We have seen that once the rate of profit in the consumers' goods industries rises beyond a certain point the system enters into an inherently unstable position : the rise of the rate of profit may for some time further stimulate investment and employment, but the effect of this must be to raise profits further till this very rise of profits leads to a curtailment of investment. This development could only be prevented if from the beginning the rate of interest rose with the rate of profit.[1] But the point at which the rate of interest might have to rise in order to prevent a further growth of investment that would lead to such an unstable position might be a phase in the recovery where there is still very considerable unemployment. Where the point of maximum stable employment which can be maintained will lie, will depend largely on what has happened during the early stages of the recovery. The " critical point " to which we have referred earlier is not a fixed point in the sense that a certain rate of investment must never be exceeded. The stage at which the expansion enters into the unstable phase will depend on a number of factors, particularly the form

has taken place, the reason why it will not pay immediately to increase investment in the other industries will probably be that there the rate of profit will be too high to make the introduction of more labour-saving methods profitable. This is therefore not a case where a discontinuity in the schedule of the marginal productivity of capital leads to a sudden fall in the returns to be expected on further investment, but a case where a (horizontal) misdirection of investment has tied up so much capital in a few industries as to create a scarcity of capital in the other industries.

[1] It should be remembered here that in this phase of the boom a general rise in money wages will only tend to raise prices and profits further and will scarcely affect real wages. A rise of money wages in the consumers' goods industries (or the late stages generally) might, however, partly counteract the rise of profits.

investment has taken during the early stages of the recovery, the rate at which investment has increased, and the rate of saving.

If the rate of profit by which investment was guided at the beginning of the recovery was very low, *i.e.*, if real wages were then comparatively high, and if in consequence investment took a form so that Q was very low and income from investment grew fast compared with the output of consumers' goods, and if in addition the rate of saving were low (or the marginal propensity to consume high), the critical point would evidently be reached sooner and the maximum of stable employment that could be attained would be comparatively low. We should have a situation where in consequence of the high real wages (or the low rate of profit) in the beginning of the recovery the limits set by the available " supply of capital " would have been exhausted by equipping fewer workmen with much capital per head : the available supply of capital would have been given such forms as if only a smaller number of men were to be permanently employed.

The maximum level of stable employment that can be reached in the short run (*i.e.*, without redistributing resources between industries) will accordingly be higher at least up to a certain point, according as :

(a) the initial rate of profit is high (or real wages low) and Q accordingly high ;

(b) the speed at which investment increases is small (which will partly be influenced by (a), because the amount of investment that will be undertaken in view of any given demand will be small, and partly by psychological factors) ; and

(c) the rate of saving is high (or the marginal propensity to consume low).

But while the ceiling of stable employment that can be reached in the short run will vary with the rate of profit ruling during the revival, this does not mean that there must be a rate of profit or a level of real wages which will lead to a stable position of *full* employment with the existing distribution of labour between industries.   There is in fact every reason to doubt whether full employment with the given distribution of labour between industries can be a stable position.[1] This distribution is the legacy of former booms, the result of the capital good industries operating in periodical spurts and supplying the consumers' goods industries by this intermittent working with all, or rather more than the equipment, which at the rate of profit that will rule under full employment it is profitable for the latter to use.   If we find that, as appears to be approximately the case, average unemployment over a whole trade cycle is in the neighbourhood of 25 per cent in the earlier stages of the capital good industries and somewhere about 10 per cent in the consumers' goods industries[2], this would mean that

[1] See on this D. H. Robertson, " A Survey of Modern Monetary Controversy," a paper read to the *Manchester Statistical Society*, 1937, p. 13.

[2] These figures are given merely as an illustration of a general tendency and make no claim to accuracy, being based on a general impression rather than a systematic study which this question would well deserve. But they are rather remarkably well borne out by figures of the mean unemployment rate (*i.e.*, the percentage of the insured males unemployed) for the period 1927-1936, which have been kindly supplied by Sir William Beveridge to the author since he used the above figures in an earlier draft of this essay. According to Sir William's calculations the mean unemployment rate during this period was 25·6 per cent for the six metal manufacture ‘ndustries of the *Labour Gazette* classification, 24·1 per cent in the

continuous full employment of all the available labour in these industries would increase the output of capital goods belonging to relatively early stages by one-third and the total output of consumers' goods by only one-ninth. And it seems clear that the consumers' goods industries could absorb such an increase in the output of capital goods only if the labour supply there were considerably increased. But so long as the capacity for producing consumers' goods is not much increased by a transfer of labour from the capital goods industries to the consumers' goods industries and an increased output of equipment capable of producing consumers' goods as against further increase of capacity for producing capital goods, all attempts to create full employment with the existing distribution of labour between industries will come up against the difficulty that with full employment people will want a larger share of the total output in the form of consumers' goods than is being produced in that form. In other words, if the last boom has come to an end because savings proved to be insufficient to maintain the rate of accumulation which full employment with the existing distribution of resources between industries implies, it is very probable that any attempt to reach full employment with the same distribution would lead to the same result.

18. *The " equilibrium " rate of profit and interest.* If too low a rate of profit during the upswing, while rapidly increasing employment in the capital good

six extractive industries other than coal mining, 24·6 per cent in coal mining, 20 per cent in the eight instrumental industries, and 20·2 per cent in the extractive, instrumental and constructional industries generally, compared with 10·1 per cent in the food, clothing and consumers' service industries.

industries where unemployment is greatest (and perhaps even further increasing the already excessive number of people attached to these industries), will make another crisis inevitable, too high a rate of profit might equally have the effect of reducing the maximum level at which employment can be lastingly maintained. While a rate that is too low may create employment in the consumers' goods industries and the capital goods industries in a proportion which corresponds to the existing distribution of labour between these industries, but will lead with full employment to a total amount of investment that cannot be maintained with the available savings, a rate that is too high might stop investment before the maximum of stable employment had been obtained.

It should be clear, then, that the dangerous mis-directions of investment will occur, that the seeds of future trouble will be sown, long before the actual " critical point " is reached, that it is the form that investment takes right from the beginning of the recovery which decides how far the expansion may be carried without making an ultimate breakdown inevitable. A policy designed to mitigate fluctuations will therefore have to watch the recovery from its very beginning. The problem is to find a middle path between the Scylla of keeping the rate of profits too low and the Charybdis of keeping it too high. The former would have the effect that profits would later rise steeply and, if expansion is allowed to continue, would lead to a crash after a period of high employ-ment in the investment good industries ; while the latter would mean that not even that maximum level of employment will be reached which can be attained in the short run and maintained afterwards without a redistribution of resources—a further increase beyond this point being only possible as savings gradually accumulate and a redistribution of labour between industries proceeds. The question is, therefore, how to find from the beginning a level of the rate of profit (and real wages) which as far as possible makes further changes in this rate unnecessary (at least changes beyond the point at which they would seriously disappoint the expectations of many people).

This " equilibrium " rate will in almost all cases be higher than the rate which will increase employment as quickly as possible, and it will also be higher than any rate which will make it possible temporarily to reach full employment with the existing distribution of labour between industries. The only way in which this short run ceiling of employment can be raised (and the " equilibrium " rate of profit lowered), it appears, is an increase in the rate of saving to a level which would allow us to accumulate capital continuously at the rate to which the existing distribution of labour between industries is adapted.

19. *Possibilities of mitigating fluctuations.* Apart from the possibility last mentioned, which is probably of importance only in the long run, our considerations suggest two ways in which the violence of industrial fluctuations might be mitigated.

In the first instance everything seems to point to the desirability of preventing the rate of profit from falling too low, and real wages from rising too high, in the later stages of the depression. While some fall of the rate of profit in the consumers' goods industries, and therefore (failing some compulsory transfer of income from consumption to investment) some reduction of incomes, seems to be necessary after the crisis, there appears to be a strong case for measures designed to prevent demand for consumers' goods and prices of consumers' goods from falling too far. Since some movement in this direction is necessary, it would delay readjustment if such measures were taken too early. And as investment and incomes begin to increase again, such extra expenditure should clearly be curtailed at the same rate. But during the later half of the decline a policy of supplementing demand by public expenditure may well be justified.

Once the rate of profit in the consumers' goods industries has already fallen too far and real wages risen too high, however, the proper remedy appears to be a reduction of wages. While, unfortunately, in the later stages of the boom a rise in money wages is not likely to have favourable effects, because it will not raise real wages, I see no reason why in the depression a reduction of money wages should not lead to a fall in real wages. And a reduction of real wages, by raising the rate of profit, will have the desired effect of preventing investments of a too capitalistic type. It will be clear on the other hand that in this situation any attempt to stimulate recovery by lowering the rate of interest below the already low rate of profit could only accentuate the later difficulties.[1]

---

[1] It may perhaps be pointed out here that it has, of course, never been denied that employment can be rapidly increased, and a position of " full employment " achieved in the shortest possible time by means of monetary expansion—least of all by those economists whose outlook has been influenced by the experience of a major inflation. All that has been contended is that the kind of full employment which can be created in this way is inherently unstable, and that to create employment by these means is to perpetuate fluctuations.

20. *The negative role of the rate of interest.* The remarks of the last section on questions of trade cycle policy have inevitably been cursory and incomplete. There arises, however, in this connection one point which is closely connected with our main problem and therefore needs more systematic consideration, namely the precise role played by the rate of interest. So far our main conclusion with respect to the rate of interest, rather borne out by recent experience, is that we might get the trade cycle even without changes in the rate of interest. We have seen that if the rate of interest fails to keep investment within the bounds determined by people's willingness to save, a rise in the rate of profit in the industries near consumption will in the end act in a way very similar to that in which the rate of interest is supposed to act, because a rise in the rate of profit beyond a certain point will bring about a decrease in investment just as an increase in the rate of interest might do.   This, of course, does not contradict the truism that a high rate of profit, if general, makes for prosperity.   There is in every situation a rate of profit which can be the same for all industries,[1] and such a uniform rate of profit throughout the system is the

There may be desperate situations in which it may indeed be necessary to increase employment at all costs, even if it be only for a short period—perhaps the situation in which Dr. Brüning found himself in Germany in 1932 was such a situation in which desperate means would have been justified.   But the economist should not conceal the fact that to aim at the maximum of employment which can be achieved in the short run by means of monetary policy is essentially the policy of the desperado who has nothing to lose and everything to gain from a short breathing space.

[1] The " same rate of profit " for the various industries means here such a position of their profit schedules that with normal employment marginal rates of profit will be the same. The statement in the text is, however, subject to the qualifications of section 17 above.

condition of a stable equilibrium. It is the function which the rate of interest is supposed to perform, but actually performs but very imperfectly, that if anywhere in the system changes in the rate of profit occur, the rates of profit are equalised at a new level by the appropriate expansions and contractions of investment in the various industries. We have seen that the operation of the rate of profit in the place of the rate of interest applies not only to the phase of expansion but also to the phase of contraction, and that it is probably the fall in the rate of profits rather than the fall in the rate of interest which in the end stimulates the introduction of more labour-saving machinery, etc., and thus revives investment. Must we conclude from this that the rate of interest is of little significance ?

This is by no means the case, although we shall probably have to conclude that its main influence is more of a negative than a positive kind ; it fails to do what in equilibrium theory it is supposed to do, and what it would have to do if equilibrium were to be preserved or rapidly to be restored after a disturbance. But failing the action of the rate of interest, other and more complicated forces come into play at a later stage and act as in pure theory the rate of interest is supposed to act. In real life the importance of the rate of interest is probably considerably greater than we have assumed here, since, while the link which connects the rate of profit and the rate of interest is very elastic, it does exist and, however tardily, the rate of interest does ultimately follow the movements of the rate of profit. For our purpose it was, however, convenient to assume that the rate of interest remained constant (or at least did not rise), in order to show that the changes which the rate of interest is supposed to bring about are not due to monetary causes but will come about even in the absence of changes in the rate of interest. The rise of the rate of profit would by itself bring the boom to an end. But in real life the rise in the rate of interest will usually bring this effect about before the rate of profit rises sufficiently.

But if in real life the rate of interest is not quite as immovable as we have assumed, its movements may yet be too tardy or too small to be effective and the rate of profit may therefore be the decisive factor. Since we know from general theoretical considerations that in order to preserve or restore equilibrium changes in the rate of interest will from time to time be necessary, all that we need to confirm the practical relevance of our argument is evidence that in real life changes in the money rate of interest are not of major significance to business men. If it can be shown that compared with the changes in the rate of profit the changes in the rate of interest are small, and that investments are actually guided, at least in many fields, much more by the rate of profit or the level of · wages than by the rate of interest, this would be the best verification of our argument that we could expect.

The familiar doubts of men of business experience about the efficacy of the rate of interest, well brought out by the recent Oxford inquiry,[1] provide considerable

---

[1] Cf. H. D. Henderson, " The Significance of the Rate of Interest," and J. E. Meade and P. W. S. Andrews, " Summary of Replies to Questions on Effects of Interest Rates," in *Oxford Economic Papers*, No. 1, October, 1938.

evidence that such is the real situation.   If in fact movements of the rate of interest follow only at a distance behind the movements of the rate of profit, and if in addition the total amplitude of fluctuations in interest rates is much smaller than the amplitude of fluctuations in the rate of profit, the rate of interest would indeed in many fields cease to be a major consideration in deciding investment policy.   But if the rate of interest fails to adjust the rate of investment to that volume which can be maintained with the available supply of " real capital " (the output of consumers' goods not consumed by its producers), the other forces which we have considered must come into play and restore the balance.

It has, of course, never been doubted, at least in more recent times, that the money rate of interest depends largely on accidental and arbitrary factors.   But if, when the rate of interest fails to follow the movements of the rate of profit, it is the rate of profit which earlier or later takes command of the situation, the factors which determine where the rate of interest actually is become much less important than the factors which determine where it ought to be.   And not only would it seem as if the importance which attaches to the question what determines the actual money rate of interest would be much smaller than is suggested by the great amount of effort and ingenuity which has recently been devoted to this question ; it also appears that manipulations of the rate of interest are of much more limited value than is often supposed because, if we try to fix it below or above its "natural level," it soon ceases to be effective.

21.   *Can the rate of interest be made effective ?* It seems
then that the idea that investment is guided by the
rate of interest is to a large extent an ideal rather than
a fact. But if it is true that under existing conditions
the rate of interest does not perform this function, or
performs it only to a very limited extent, this does not
mean that it cannot or that it ought not to be made
to do so. And it does not even necessarily mean that
in order to make the rate of interest more effective its
movements would have to be bigger than they are
to-day. Even if there are many considerations which
make it plausible that the initiating power of
spontaneous changes in the rate of interest is comparatively small, these considerations do not necessarily
apply to its power to offset changes in the rate of profit.
If it is mainly changes which affect his current business
which make an entrepreneur look round and revise
his plans, it may well be that he is fairly indifferent to
such spontaneous changes in the rate of interest, but
quite sensitive at the moment when changes in his
profits make him think of altering his investment
policy.

We must not forget that the rise (and similarly the
fall) of the rate of profit only becomes so big as it
actually does because, failing a parallel movement of
the rate of interest, a rise of profits will for a considerable
period further stimulate investment of all kinds. And
while, once this process has gone some distance, the
rise in the rate of interest required to check it might
indeed be very considerable, a prompt adjustment of
the rate of interest as soon as profits begin to rise (or
fall), although not involving a great change, might

well be effective.[1] While changes in the rate of interest within the customary range may be quite powerless at the date at which, because of the delay action of our credit mechanism, they now take place, their effect might be quite sufficient to preserve a reasonable equilibrium if they were made promptly. It is even probable that the total amplitude of the changes in the rate of interest required would be smaller than the fluctuations observed in the past if only they followed more promptly upon changes in the rate of profit.

What amount of changes in the rate of interest would be necessary to prevent the recurrence of cumulative processes in either direction we do not know because such a policy has never been tried.[2] And it is, of course, true that in the absence of an automatic mechanism making rates of interest move with rates of profits it would require superhuman wisdom to adjust them perfectly by deliberate policy. But this by no means proves that we might not get much nearer to the ideal than we have ever done. It is, *e.g.*, evidently an anomaly which indicates inflationary developments that in almost all past booms the prices of fixed interest

[1] It is no contradiction to argue that investments in the individual firm are guided not so much by the rate of interest as by the rate of profit, and at the same time to advocate the use of the rate of interest as a means to control investment. Although a rise of the rate of interest may have little effect on the proportional amount of capital used by particular firms, it will, by reducing the total amount of production in the early stages where profits have not risen, reduce the amount of investment for industry as a whole.

[2] An exception should probably be made for the action of the Federal Reserve Board in the spring of 1923, when by raising the rates of interest they brought an incipient boom to an end and caused a merely slight and short recession, soon followed by a rapid revival. But this policy was unfortunately abandoned and actually reversed on the next occasion in 1927, with the fatal consequences we all know.

securities have been allowed to rise (*i.e.*, the long term
rate of interest has been allowed to fall) for some time
after industrial profits have already begun to move
upwards. It seems clear that such a development ought
to be prevented by a timely increase of the money rate
of interest. Actual developments of policy, particularly
in recent times, have, however, been in the opposite
direction ; the tendency to keep the rates of interest
stable, and especially to keep them low as long as
possible, must appear as the arch-enemy of stability,
causing in the end much greater fluctuations, probably
even of the rate of interest, than are really necessary.[1]
Perhaps it should be repeated that this applies especially
to the doctrine, now so widely accepted, that interest
rates should be kept low till " full employment " in
general is reached. While it appears that we can have
the trade cycle without changes in the rate of interest
we shall probably never have a reasonable degree of
stability without such changes.

If we have to steer a car along a narrow road between
two walls, we can either keep it in the middle of the

[1] This has, of course, been argued again and again by economists
ever since the beginning of last century. To mention only one
author who has been rather neglected in the recent historical surveys
of these discussions, H. D. Macleod (*The Theory and Practice of
Banking*, Vol. II, 1st ed. 1856, pp. 371-2, 3rd ed. 1879, p. 273)
wrote : " We may feel quite certain that if during the various crises
this country has passed through, there had been more attention paid
to observe the natural rate of discount, instead of thwarting the
course of nature, though variations would have been more frequent,
they would have been less violent and extreme. . . . Such, however,
is the perversity of men, that many think that a uniform and
invariable rate of discount is the great thing to be preserved, no
matter what nature may say to the contrary, and their ingenuity is
racked to devise a plan for always keeping it so, just as if the
governor of a steam engine ought always to revolve with uniform
velocity."

road by fairly frequent but small movements of the steering wheel ; or we can wait longer when the car deviates to one side and then bring it back by more or less violent jerks, probably overshooting the mark and risking collision with the other wall ; or we can try to keep the steering wheel stiff and let the car bang alternately into either wall with a good chance of leading the car and ourselves to ultimate destruction.

II

INVESTMENT THAT RAISES THE DEMAND FOR CAPITAL[1]

THE purpose of this essay is to state a proposition which underlies the modern " monetary over-invest-ment theories " of the trade cycle in a form in which, as far as I know, it has never before been expressed, but which seems to make this particular proposition so obvious as to put its logical correctness beyond dispute. This, of course, does not necessarily mean that the theories which rely largely on this proposition provide an adequate account of all or any trade cycles. But it should do something to show the inadequacies of those current theories which completely disregard the effect in question. It should, moreover, clear up some of the confusion and misunderstandings which have made it so difficult to come to an agreement on the purely analytical points involved.

It will surprise nobody to find the source of this confusion in the ambiguity of the term capital. In static analysis, the term capital refers equally to the aggregate value of all capital goods and to their "quantity," measured in terms of cost (or in some other way). But this is of little significance because in

Reprinted from *The Review of Economic Statistics*, Vol. XIX, No. 4, November, 1937.

equilibrium these two magnitudes must necessarily coincide.   In the analysis of dynamic phenomena, however, this ambiguity becomes exceedingly dangerous.   In particular, the static proposition that an increase in the quantity of capital will bring about a fall in its marginal productivity (which for the purposes of this article I shall call the rate of interest), when taken over into economic dynamics and applied to the quantity of capital goods, may become quite definitely erroneous.

1. *The Relative Significance of the Amount of Investment and of the Form that it takes*

The assumption that an increase in the quantity of capital goods will necessarily decrease the return to be expected on further investment is generally treated as obvious.   It is, therefore, desirable to state the actual relations between the two magnitudes in a form which may, perhaps, sound somewhat paradoxical.   The main thesis of this article will be that the effect which the current production of capital goods will have on the future demand for investible funds will depend not so much on the quantity of capital goods produced, as on the kind of capital goods which are produced or on the particular forms which current investment takes, and that an increase in the current output of capital goods will frequently have the effect not of lowering but of raising the future demand for investible funds, and thereby the rate of interest.

Each separate step of the argument which leads to this conclusion is a familiar and obvious proposition.

The first main point is that most investment is undertaken in the expectation that further investment, for which the equipment that formed the object of the first investment will be needed, will take place at a later date. This may be expressed by saying that current investment will be guided by the expectation that investment will continue at a certain rate for some time to come, or that the rate of interest will stay at a certain figure. The success of current investment will depend upon this expectation being fulfilled. Most individual acts of investment must be regarded, therefore, as mere links in a chain which has to be completed if its parts are to serve the function for which they were intended, even though the chain consists of separate and successive acts of different entrepreneurs. The manufacturer of any kind of machines who increases his plant can do so only in the expectation that the users of these machines will at some later time be willing to install additional machines, and that these machines may be wanted only if somebody else will later be willing to invest in their products, etc., etc.

The first investment of such a chain, therefore, will be undertaken only if it is expected that in each link of this chain a certain rate of interest can be earned. But this does not mean that, *once this investment has been made*, the process of further investments will not be continued if conditions change in an unfavourable direction—if, for example, the rate of interest at which money can be borrowed rises. If the investments already made are irrevocably committed to the particular purpose, this provides a margin within which the total profits to be expected on the whole chain of successive investments may fall without affecting the profitability of the further investments still needed to complete the process. For if the fixed capital already created is specific to the particular purpose, it will, of course, be used even if the return covers little more than the cost of using it (but not interest and amortisation) ; and since the owners of this fixed capital will find it in their interest to use it so long as they get only a little more than mere operating cost, nearly the whole amount which it was originally expected would be earned as interest and amortisation becomes available, as it were, as a premium on investment in the later stages of the process. The amount by which entrepreneurs in these later stages need to pay less for the products of the earlier stages, because the equipment there is already in existence, thus becomes available for expenditure on the completion of the process. And the greater the amount of investment which has already been made compared with that which is still required to utilise the equipment already in existence, the greater will be the rate of interest which can advantageously be borne in raising capital for these investments completing the chain.

2. *"Completing Investments" and the Rate of Interest*

Obviously then, the demand for capital at any particular moment depends not so much on the productivity that the existing structure of real capital

would have if completed—the long term schedule of
the productivity of investment—as on the proportion
between that part of it which has already been
completed and that part which has yet to be added to
complete it. Only for a very small fraction of the total
investments—the marginal investments which represent
the beginning of new chains of investment—will the
demand for funds promptly react to a change in the
rate at which capital can be borrowed. For the rest,
the demand for capital will be highly inelastic with
respect to changes in the rate of interest.

The consequences of this can readily be shown by a
schematic example. Assume that past investments
have been guided by the expectation that a rate of
interest of 4 per cent would continue to rule for some
time, but that in order to complete the investments
which have been undertaken in this expectation a
greater supply of loanable funds would be required than
is actually forthcoming. Assume further that, if
investments in the recent past had been guided by the
expectation of a 5 per cent rate of interest, the amount
of further loans required to continue these investment
processes would just exhaust the current supply. This
does not mean that once investments have been undertaken in the expectation of a rate of 4 per cent, a rise
of the interest rate to 5 per cent—that is, to the figure
which, if correctly foreseen, would have represented an
equilibrium rate—will now be sufficient to reduce
demand for loans to the level of the supply. If a
considerable part of the equipment to be used has
already been produced, many investments, which it
would never have been profitable to start if a rate of

interest of 5 per cent had been foreseen, will be well worth while continuing, even at a rate much higher than 5 per cent. The loss will fall entirely on those entrepreneurs who in the past, in the expectation of the lower rate of interest, have already erected new plant, etc. But the concessions in price, below their actual cost of production, which they will be compelled to make, will enable the other entrepreneurs, whom they supply with equipment, to go on with the installation of new machinery, which would not have been possible if developments had been foreseen correctly from the outset. The construction of a large hydro-electric plant that would have been profitable if the rate of interest had remained at 4 per cent will prove unprofitable if the rate of interest rises. But, once it has been constructed and charges for electric power adjusted to get maximum profit over current expenditure, it will give rise to a further demand for capital for the installation of electric motors, etc., which will not be sensibly reduced even by a rate of interest much higher than 5 per cent.[1]

How far the rate of interest will have to rise to bring the demand for loans down to the available supplies will depend, as we have seen, on the proportion between that part of the complete investment processes which had been carried out before the unexpected rise in the rate of interest occurred, and that part of this total expenditure which has yet to be incurred. If, in a particular instance, interest at 4 per cent on the capital already invested and amortisation of that capital would have represented 30 per cent of the

---

[1] Cf. my *Monetary Theory and the Trade Cycle*, 1933, p. 224 f.

expected price of the final commodity in the production of which it was to be used, then interest charges involved in utilising the existing plant and its products would have to rise so as to absorb the whole of this 30 per cent of the final price, before the demand for capital for this purpose would be effectively curtailed. If, of the remaining 70 per cent of the expected total cost of the final product, 15 per cent was allowed for further interest at 4 per cent, interest rates would have to rise to approximately 12 per cent before the profitability of the investments completing the process already begun would be reduced to zero.

Against this whole argumentation it might be objected that it completely ignores the effect of the rise in interest rates on current replacement of the capital in the " earlier stages " which has partly or entirely lost its value. It is certainly true that these items of equipment will not be replaced. But the implication that this will in any way relieve the demand for funds for investment is certainly erroneous. In so far as those items in the normal course of affairs would already need replacement, these replacements would have been financed out of amortisation currently earned. They would not have constituted a demand on the funds available for investments. But if—and this is more likely—they have not yet become ripe for replacement, the amortisation earned would temporarily be available for investment elsewhere. The fact that no amortisation or only a reduced quota will be earned will then mean a reduction of the supply of investible funds, that is, it will represent a factor which tends to raise rather than lower the rate of interest.

3. Causes of an Urgent Demand for Funds for Completing Investments

The causes which are likely to bring about such a situation remain to be considered. Under what conditions will the demand for the additional capital required to complete a given capital structure drive up the rate of interest to a figure very much higher than the rate which is compatible with the permanent maintenance of that structure?

In principle the answer is surely clear. Anything which will lead people to expect a lower rate of interest, or a larger supply of investible funds, than will actually exist when the time comes for their utilisation, will in the way we have suggested force interest rates to rise much higher than would have been the case if people had not expected such a low rate. But, while it is true that an unexpected decrease in the rate of saving, or an unforeseen appearance of a new demand for capital— a new invention for instance—may bring about such a situation, the most important cause practically of such false expectations probably is a temporary increase in the supply of such funds through credit expansion at a rate which cannot be maintained. In this case, the increased quantity of current investment will induce people to expect investment to continue at a similar rate for some time, and in consequence to invest now in a form which requires for its successful completion further investment at a similar rate.[1] It

[1] For a somewhat fuller statement of these connections see my articles "Preiserwartungen, monetäre Störungen und Fehlinvestitionen," *Nationalökonomisk Tidsskrift*, Vol. 73/3 (1935) (also a French version in the *Revue des Sciences Economiques*, Liège, October, 1935), and " The Maintenance of Capital," *Economica*, II

is not so much the quantity of current investment but the direction it takes—the *type* of capital goods being produced—which determines the amount of future investment required if the current investments are to be successfully incorporated in the structure of production. But it is the amount of investment made possible by the current supply of funds which determines expectations about the future rate of investment and thereby the form that the current investment will be given. We can now see the justification for the somewhat paradoxical form in which the main thesis of this article was originally stated. An increase in the rate of investment, or the quantity of capital goods, may have the effect of raising rather than lowering the rate of interest, if this increase has given rise to the expectation of a greater future supply of investible funds than is actually forthcoming.

If this proposition is correct, and if its assumptions are empirically justified, this means that much of the purely monetary analysis of the trade cycle now current is built on very insufficient foundations. If it is correct, the common assumption that the expected return on investment, or the " marginal efficiency of capital," can be treated as a simple decreasing function of the quantity of capital goods in existence, or of the current rate of investment, will have to be abandoned, and with it much of the argument based on the supposed tendency of the " marginal efficiency of capital " to fall more rapidly than the money rate of interest. If past investment is often found to make further investment more

(New series, August, 1935), particularly pp. 268 *et seq.* [These two articles are now reprinted below as numbers 4 and 3 of the present collection pp. 83 and 135.]

rather than less profitable, this would also mean that the rise of the rate of interest towards the end of a boom—which so many authors believe can be explained only by *monetary* factors affecting the *supply* of loanable funds—can be adequately explained by *real* factors affecting the *demand*. It shows, moreover, that a purely monetary analysis, which runs in terms of mere rates of investment without analysing the concrete structure of these investments and the influence which monetary factors can have on this real structure of production, is bound to neglect some of the most significant elements in the picture. And, perhaps, it also explains why a careful analysis of the time structure of production (*not* in terms of an " average " period of production) is a necessary basis for a satisfactory analysis of the trade cycle.

III

THE MAINTENANCE OF CAPITAL[1]

1. *The nature and significance of the problem.* It is not likely that in the whole field of economics there are many more concepts which are at the same time so generally used and so little analysed as that of a " constant amount of capital." But while in the investigation of the effects of nearly any change this is almost without exception treated as a given datum, the question what this assumption exactly means is rarely asked. To most economists the answer to it has apparently seemed so simple and obvious that they have never attempted to state it. In consequence the difficulties involved have hardly ever been realised, still less have they been adequately investigated.

The difficulties of the problem would undoubtedly have been realised if economists had been more generally conscious of its importance. But although, even in the analysis of a stationary equilibrium, the inclusion of the "quantity of capital" among the determinants of that equilibrium means that something which is the result of the equilibrating process, is treated as if it were a datum,[2] this confusion was made

---

[1] Reprinted from *Economica*, Vol. II. (N.S.) August, 1935.
[2] Cf. K. Wicksell, *Lectures on Political Economy*, Vol. I, p. 202. London, 1934.

relatively innocuous by the essential limitations of the static method, which while it describes the conditions of a state of equilibrium, does not explain how such a state is brought about.

It was only with the more modern attempts to make the descriptions of the conditions of equilibrium the basis of the analysis of the dynamic processes, that the exact meaning of this assumption became of serious consequence.   But we need not go far beyond the description of one state of equilibrium to see why it matters.   Even the very simplest " problem of variation " as the effect of a shift in demand can only be answered on the basis of a definite assumption as regards the " supply of capital," and the usual answer shows immediately how problematic is the assumption on which it rests.

The idea implicit in the discussion of problems of this sort is that there is a quantitatively determined fund of capital, which can be distributed and redistributed in any way between the different lines of production without changing its aggregate value.[1]   But has this assumption of a perfectly mobile capital fund any definite meaning ?   And if so, what determines whether this value remains constant, what are the conditions under which it will remain constant, how is it measured, and by what is this constant magnitude represented ? Certainly not by the concrete capital goods.   It is the

---

[1] This common assumption has recently been stated with particular emphasis by Professor Pigou in his latest article on the subject to be quoted later.   He finds the basis of his deductions " in the concept of capital as an entity capable of maintaining its quantity while altering its form and by its nature always drawn to those forms on which, so to speak, the sun of profit is at the time shining." *Economic Journal*, June, 1935, p. 239.

essential difference between them and factors like labour or land that they will not remain physically the same when prices change, but that the physical composition of the aggregate called capital will change in consequence of any change in the data. Any of the problems of variation with which we are concerned will involve what is commonly called a transformation of capital into other forms. It is not the list of the different pieces of individual capital goods which is assumed to remain unchanged, when we speak of a constant supply of capital, in the same way as we assume that the total supply of labour or land is composed of elements of the same kind, when we regard its supply as unchanged.

Even if a definite meaning can be attached to the statement that the value of the capital goods has an existence independent of the capital goods themselves, it does not help us in any way to explain why, or under what conditions, this aggregate value should remain constant, when conditions change. There can be no doubt that the value of at least some of the existing capital goods will be very materially affected by almost any conceivable change. The question then is why should the capitalists, in spite of this change in the value of their concrete capital goods, be able and willing, by an appropriate adjustment of their investment activity, to maintain the total value of their possessions at exactly the same figure as before the change. Is there any justification for considering this in any sense to be the " normal " behaviour of the entrepreneurs, or is it even conceivable that they can, under all circumstances, behave in such a way ? Must we not rather assume that under some conditions it will be impossible for the capitalist to maintain the value of his capital constant, while under others it could hardly be considered in any sense " normal " if he did no more than this ?

What, then, is that neutral state in which the owners of capital are supposed to take a merely passive attitude performing no new saving or dissaving ? This question, already of considerable importance when we try to trace the consequences of any other change, becomes of special importance when we turn to the autonomous changes which can be said to originate on the side of capital. Then already the initial problem, of what can be regarded as such an autonomous change on the side of capital, depends on our definition of that neutral state. In the usual discussions of this sort of problem, it seems to be generally implied that there is a clear line between the normal process of maintaining and replacing the existing capital, and any net addition to it. It is assumed that it is always possible to decide in an unequivocal way whether capital remains constant, increases, or decreases, and that there are typical phenomena connected with each of these processes which, at least conceptually, can be clearly separated. Indeed, so long as all the other data remain constant, no difficulty arises in this connection. But as soon as one tries to apply these categories to a world where things are changing, all these alluringly simple concepts become dependent in more than one way on exactly what is meant by a given stock of capital. It is impossible to define income (or " earnings ") and therefore savings before one has separated from the gross produce those quantities which are required to " maintain " capital, and it is equally impossible to say what are additions to the stock of real capital before one has shown what capital goods are required to make up for current depreciation.

If it should prove that serious difficulties arise in this connection, this would be a matter of great importance for the theory of the trade cycle. In the course of the last generation theorists in that field have tended more and more to agree that industrial fluctuations consist essentially in alternating periods of accumulation and decumulation of capital with all their typical consequences. More recently there has seemed to be considerable unanimity in seeking for causes of these fluctuations in the accumulation of capital in conditions which make the movement of investment to a certain extent independent of that of saving. But although the quantitative relationship between saving and investing, their correspondence or non-correspondence, has become the central point of attack, it seems that all the writers who have made use of that approach have failed to make clear exactly what they meant either by saving or investing. This would have required a careful definition of that neutral position in which neither positive nor negative saving were made, because all the income and no more than the income was consumed, and in which capital goods were produced in exactly that quantity and composition that is required to keep the stock of capital intact.

But while it cannot be denied that modern trade cycle theorists (including the present writer) have lamentably failed to provide a concept which is indeed indispensable if their deductions are to have a clear meaning, it seems that they are not the only group of economists who have been deceived by the apparent simplicity of the problem. Even more than this group one should expect the writers on the income concepts to have provided a clear answer. And even if the general discussions of the income concept should prove disappointing, one would certainly feel entitled to expect a definite answer in the discussions of business profits, since profits of all things can evidently only be defined as the excess of the total business assets over the equivalent of the capital invested at the beginning of the period. But while we find in general discussions of the income concept, particularly in the writings of Professor Irving Fisher,[1] at least some references to our problem, the standard works on business profits, like Professor F. H. Knight's *Risk, Uncertainty, and Profits*, or Mr. C. O. Hardy's *Risk and Risk Bearing*, are almost bare of any reference to the problem.

2. *Professor Pigou's treatment.* In view of these circumstances the solitary attempt first made by Professor Pigou a few years ago in the third edition of his *Economics of Welfare* deserves far greater attention than it has actually received. Although Professor Pigou discusses the problem for a special purpose, the definition of a national dividend, he raises most of the problems that need investigation. And it is only an additional reason for gratitude to that distinguished author that he has apparently not felt satisfied with his first attempt towards an answer and that he has in the fourth edition of the same work given us an

---

[1] By his definition of income, which identifies it with actual consumption, I. Fisher seems to avoid the problem altogether. But it recurs in connection with his concept of earnings, which corresponds to the ordinary income concept. And although he does not provide an explicit answer, the solution of the problem which seems to be implied in his discussion, or at least the only solution which seems to be consistent with it, appears to be very much the same as that attempted in this paper.

entirely new version of his solution.[1] In the third edition he had still considered that the problem could simply and only be answered by " employing money values in some way as our measuring rod," but that we cannot employ crude money values but must introduce " corrections."[2] Accordingly, he defined as constant quantities of capital collections of capital goods, whose aggregate money value, divided by an appropriate index number of general prices, remained constant. After making some further allowances for changes in this magnitude caused by changes in the rate of interest, which need not concern us here, he proceeded to apply this definition to cases where the value of capital goods " is destroyed through a failure of demand or through a new discovery which renders existing instruments obsolete,"[3] and suggests, consistently with the criterion adopted, that in such a case it is convenient, although arbitrary, to say that the stock of capital has decreased (or in the reverse case of an expansion of demand that it has increased).

In the fourth edition of the *Economics of Welfare* the entire chapter is rewritten.   Although no explicit explanation is given why the former answer has been abandoned, it is fairly evident from the nature of the changes made, and the general shift of emphasis, that the aim has been to make the decision more dependent on the reasons why it is thought desirable to maintain capital intact. Considerations relating to the constancy

---

[1] Since this paper has been completed a further study of this problem has been published by Professor Pigou under the title " Net Income and Capital Depletion " (*Economic Journal*, June, 1935). Some references to this paper will be made in further footnotes.

[2] *Economics of Welfare*, 3rd Ed. (1929), p. 45.

[3] *Economics of Welfare*, 3rd Ed., p. 47.

of the money value of capital which formerly occupied the chief place are now relegated to a subordinate place, and mentioned only to show that if, all other things remaining the same, in consequence of a contraction in the supply of money, money values all round are substantially reduced, and the money value of capital contracts along with the rest, nobody would consider this as a decrease of capital. The second case mentioned is again that of the effects of a change in the rate of interest on the value of capital, and it is decided (apparently on the assumption that such a change will not affect the return from the existing capital goods) that such changes are not to be considered as changes in the quantity of capital, so far as the estimation of the national dividend is concerned. But then the effects of changes in demand and of inventions are taken up, and here the decision is now the reverse from what it was before. In Professor Pigou's opinion, " we may say quite generally that all contractions in the money value of any part of the capital stock that remains physically unaltered are irrelevant to the national dividend ; and that their occurrence is perfectly compatible with the maintenance of capital intact."[1] The same applies to actual destruction of the capital goods by " acts of God or the King's enemy," where the distinguishing criterion is that they are not incidental to the use of them, or as I shall suggest instead, because and in so far as they cannot be

---

[1] *Ibid.*, 4th Ed. (1932), p. 45. In his latest article on the subject Professor Pigou goes even further and suggests that also physical changes which, while leaving a capital good as productive as ever, bring nearer the day of sudden and final breakdown, should be disregarded in the same way as the nearer approach of the day that will make it obsolete (*Economic Journal*, p. 238).

foreseen.[1] But all other physical deterioration in the capital stock, such as the ordinary wear and tear of machinery and plant, destruction by accidents like fire and storm, in so far as these are, as in the case of ships, incidental to their use, ought to be made good by adding " to the capital stock something whose value is equal to that which the machine, had it remained physically intact, would have now."[2] By this are explicitly excluded all the losses in value, which are not due to physical deterioration, but are due to causes like the changes in demand or the new inventions mentioned before, to which Professor Pigou now adds foreign competition. This is expressly confirmed by the concluding sentence of the paragraph, in which, summarising the result, he says, " Maintenance of capital intact for our purposes means then, not replacement of all value losses (not due to acts of God and the King's enemies), but replacement of such value losses as are caused by physical losses other than the above."[3]

We shall have to discuss these cases in greater detail in the systematic part of this article. Here only one

---

[1] In his recent article (p. 240), Professor Pigou now suggests the same distinction.

[2] *Economics of Welfare*, 4th Ed., p. 47.

[3] *Ibid.* In the latest version of his views, to which reference has been made in the preceding footnotes, Professor Pigou now regards it as necessary in order to make good the depletion of capital implied in the discarding of a capital good, that a quantity of resources be engaged in the production of a new capital good which would suffice in actual current conditions of technique to reproduce the discarded element (*loc. cit.*, p. 239). Professor Pigou seems to overlook here the fact that " in actual current conditions of technique " it may be much more expensive to reproduce the identical capital good than it either was when it was first produced or than it would be to replace it by a much more up-to-date instrument. It would certainly be much more expensive to reproduce a new 1926 model of a car to replace one that is worn out, than to replace it by a 1935 model.

difficulty arising out of Professor Pigou's answer may be mentioned, since it opens up the vista on a set of problems which he has left untouched. What seems most surprising in his classification is that obsolescence, even where it is foreseen at the time a capital good is produced or acquired, and where accordingly the investment is made in the expectation that the product will cease to have value long before it has physically decayed, should not have to be made good in order to maintain capital intact. This means that gradually all existing capital may be squandered, in the ordinary sense, by erecting durable structures for very transient purposes, and replacing them, when they become obsolete after a short time, only by capital goods of a value equal to that which they still possess after their temporary utility has passed. Surely there must be some cases where obsolescence, a decrease of usefulness of a capital good not connected with any change in its physical condition, has to be taken into account. And apparently, the distinction must somehow be based on whether that change can be foreseen or not. But if this is so, does it not provide a criterion of much more general use than the casuistic distinctions drawn by Professor Pigou ? This is the problem to which we have to turn.[1]

3. *The* Rationale *of maintaining capital intact.* To " maintain capital intact " is not an aim in itself. It

[1] Professor Pigou's views on the subject have recently been discussed in some detail in two Italian articles by A. M. Neuman (Osservazioni sul concetto di " capitale inalterato." e sulla recente formulazione del prof. Pigou) and F. Vito (La nozione di lunghezza media del processo produttivo) in the *Rivista Internazionale di Scienze Sociale e Discipline Ausiliare*, Anno XLI, Serie III, September, 1933 (Vol. IV, fasc. V), and by R. F. Fowler, *The Depreciation of Capital*, London, 1934, pp. 14–21.

is only desired because of certain consequences which are known to follow from a failure to do so. And as we shall see, it is not even possible to attach a definite sense to this phrase if we try to apply it to a changing world, independently of why we want to do so. We are not interested in its magnitude because there is any inherent advantage in any particular absolute measurement of capital, but only because, *ceteris paribus*, a change in this magnitude would be a cause of a change in the income to be expected from it, and because in consequence *every* change in its magnitude may be a symptom for such a change in the really relevant magnitude, income. Professor Pigou has abandoned the attempt to define in terms of a value dimension of capital the position, in which the stock of capital undergoes no changes that need to be added to or deducted from the output of consumers' goods for the computation of the national dividend. He has thereby not only acknowledged the inherent difficulties of any value measurement, which in the present case indeed are particularly serious,[1] but he has apparently also recognised the much more fundamental fact that such constancy of the value dimension has no necessary connection with the reasons why we wish to " maintain

---

[1] In the case of the comparison of different money incomes of a person or a group of persons, the result of a computation of an index number can be given a definite meaning, if the index number is constructed in such a way as to show that the one income would buy all that could be bought with the other income *plus* something else, or that it will not buy all that can be obtained with the other income. (On all this cf. G. Haberler, *Der Sinn der Indexzahlen, passim*, and J. M. Keynes, *A Treatise on Money*, Book II.) But it must appear very doubtful whether there are any assumptions on which price levels, not only of consumers' goods, but of all goods composing the stock of capital, *i.e.*, of all goods of any description, can be given a similar meaning.

capital intact," and that in consequence there is no reason to assume that people will in fact normally act in such a way as to keep the value of the stock of capital constant.[1]

What, then, are the reasons why we wish capital to behave in a particular way ? In the first instance, this reason is evidently that the persons who draw an income from capital, want to avoid using up unintentionally parts of the source of this income, which must be preserved if income is to be kept at the present level. We want to avoid an unintentional temporary " splashing " or " stinting " which would have the effect of later reducing income below or raising it above the level at which we aim. Capital accounting in this sense is simply a technical device, an abbreviated method of solving the complicated problems arising out of this task of avoiding involuntary infringements upon future income. Whatever the time shape of the future income stream derived from the capital in his possession at which an individual aims, there still remains the problem of deciding what is the required action with regard to the individual parts of his possessions. And although we have certainly no right to assume that every person will normally aim at a permanent constant stream of income from his capital, there is probably some justification for regarding this case as one of special interest. In any case, even when the capitalist aims at some other shape of the income stream, the problem remains the same, and

[1] Professor Pigou's treatment of the problem in his recent article seems, however, to some extent rather a return to a much earlier materialist conception which sees in capital some physical substance whose magnitude is independent not only of its money value, but also of its serviceability.

the case of the constant income stream might simply be regarded as the standard with which the other cases are compared.

So long as we confine ourselves to the effects of the decisions of the capitalist on his own income stream, it may seem arbitrary to treat any one of the different sets of consistent decisions regarding his future income stream as in any way more " normal " than any other. It may even have a certain theoretical attraction simply to define whatever incomes he wants to have at different periods as equal incomes. We are, however, constrained by other reasons to abstain from such a pure subjectivism and to adopt a more objective standard. These other reasons are that we are interested in the maintenance of capital, not only because of the people who themselves deliberately distribute income over time and by so doing become capitalists, but also because of the effect of their activity on the incomes of other people. In the case of the workman, whose labour receives a greater remuneration because of the co-operation of capital, but who is not himself an owner of capital, we have no expression of his preference as regards the shape of his income stream, and we have to *assume* that he wants an income stream which does at least not decrease. Such a constant income stream in an objective sense might provisionally be defined as consisting at every successive moment of varying collections of commodities actually bought at an aggregate price, at which the collection of commodities actually bought at the beginning of the period might have been obtained.

4. *The action of the capitalist with perfect foresight.* The next task, then, is to find out how the individual

owner of capital goods will behave, if he wants to keep the income he derives from his possessions constant, and if he has complete foresight of all relevant changes.[1] Complete foresight in this sense need not refer to all the relevant future. It is sufficient for our purpose to assume that at any one moment he foresees all changes that will affect the return of the investment he then makes. His anticipation need only be correct for a period equal to that for which his investment runs, and if he makes investments in different fields, the extent of his foresight need only cover the relevant facts affecting the different investments during such different periods as these investments last. Beyond this, only some more general expectation as regards the rate of interest at which it will be possible to reinvest the capital recovered, will be necessary.

Within these periods, his anticipations must in the first instance cover the relevant price changes. But such

[1] It is, of course, not assumed that the capitalist under consideration has always possessed complete foresight, since in this case the problem of adaptation of his plans to an anticipated change would not arise. All that is assumed is that at a given moment all future changes relevant to his investments become known to him. The difficulties which any such assumption of foresight of all relevant changes involves are well known. The only way in which such foresight, not only of the real changes, but of all prices during the relevant period, is conceivable is that all these prices are actually fixed simultaneously in advance on some single market, where not only present but also all future commodities that will become available during the relevant period are traded. This introduces the further difficulty that to fulfil the condition it would be necessary that the periods for which people foresee are the same for all individuals, and that the changes that will happen in the more distant future are disclosed periodically and simultaneously to all people. However, it is not necessary here to go further into all the difficulties raised by this assumption, which will be dropped later, difficulties which are by no means exhausted by those mentioned. Attention had to be drawn to them only in order to make us realise how unreal the assumption of perfect foresight is (even for the limited periods relevant to our problem).

foreknowledge is hardly conceivable without some foresight of the real changes, which bring about the changes in prices. The main types of changes, which he will have to foresee and the effects of which we shall have to discuss, will be changes in the demand for the products and the consequent changes, not only of the prices of the products, but also of the prices of the factors, changes in the quantities of the factors of production, and changes in their prices caused in this way (including, in particular, in both these cases, changes in the rate of interest), and finally, changes of technical knowledge or inventions. With respect to this last case the idea of foresight evidently presents some difficulty, since an invention which has been foreseen in all details would not be an invention. All we can here assume is that people anticipate that the process used now will at some definite date be superseded by some new process not yet known in detail. But this degree of knowledge may be sufficient to limit investments in the kind of equipment, which is bound to be made obsolete by the expected invention, in such a way that the old equipment wears out as the new invention can be introduced.

If we take first the case of an anticipated change in the demand, either away from or towards the product produced by our capitalist, his knowledge of this impending change, a full investment period in advance of its actual occurrence, will evidently put him in a position so to redistribute the earned amortisation quotas of his capital between the different industries that he will derive the greatest return from them possible under the new conditions. But in what sense will these amortisation quotas represent a constant magnitude, and under what conditions can we assume that the capitalist will invest them and no more and no less, if he merely aims at keeping his income from capital from now onwards constant ?

There is no reason to assume that, if he just continues to reinvest, after the change has become known, the amounts he used to invest, in what appears the most profitable way in the light of the new knowledge, this will have that effect. The shift in demand between different products, if the co-efficients of production in the different lines of industry are not exactly the same, is bound to change the relative prices of the factors, and these changes will occur gradually as all the entrepreneurs redirect their resources in anticipation of the impending change. If we take the simplest imaginable case where there is only one uniform scarce factor besides " capital," namely labour, it will depend on the relative quantities of labour required in the lines of industry, to and from which demand is expected to shift, whether the product of labour invested for longer periods will fall relatively to that of labour invested for shorter periods, or vice versa.

If we assume that the industry, whose product will be in stronger demand, is one where relatively more capital is required, the tendency will be for wages to fall, and prospective returns on capital to rise. The way in which this is brought about is that, out of the amortisation quotas shifted to the industry now more favoured by demand, the capitalist will be willing to pay only wages corresponding to the lower marginal productivity of labour there. And since the withdrawal of these amortisation quotas from the other industry will decrease demand for labour there, wages will gradually fall.

The position of the capitalist will thereby be affected in a double way. The gradual fall of wages will leave in his hands a greater amount of gross profits to be divided between investment and consumption. And the expected returns on the reinvestment of these receipts will be increased. How much of these gross receipts from capital will he have to reinvest, if he wants to obtain a constant income stream from that moment onwards? There are three main types of possible reactions of which only one corresponds to that criterion. Either he may go on, until the change has actually occurred, to consume only as much as before. In that case he will have invested during the period constantly increasing amounts of money, and will consequently find himself at the end of the period in possession of a greater stock of capital, which will probably give him a greater percentage return (on the assumption that all other entrepreneurs act in the same way, but that the consequent increase of capital will not lead to proportionally greater reduction of interest, *i.e.*, that the elasticity of the demand for capital under the new conditions is greater than unity). In this case his net income would at the end of the transition period suddenly increase, a change which does not correspond to the postulate that income should remain constant from the moment when the impending change becomes known.

Or we may assume that during the transition period he continues to reinvest amortisation quotas of the same magnitude as before. In this case his expenditure on consumers' goods will gradually increase during the transition period as the rate of interest increases, his capital will remain the same in money value, and will give him from the moment the anticipated change has actually occurred onwards, a permanently higher income. This again clearly does not correspond to the assumption that he disposes of his resources in such a way, that in the light of his knowledge he may at every moment expect a constant income stream.

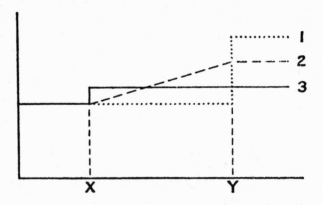

To do so he would have to raise his consumption, at the moment the impending change becomes known, to a level at which it can be permanently maintained. This implies that during the transition period he will increase his consumption and reduce his reinvestment to such a figure that at the end of the period he will be in possession of a quantity of capital which, although in every conceivable dimension it may be smaller than that he owned before, will at the higher rate of interest give him an income equal to that enjoyed during the transition period, and higher than that which he had before the change became known.

These alternative policies of the capitalist can easily be depicted by means of a diagram. The alternative income streams are here represented by the lines marked 1, 2, and 3 respectively. The ordinate for every point of the abscissa, on which time is measured, represents the magnitude of the income stream at that moment. The change is supposed to occur at Y, and to be first foreseen at X (which precedes Y by at least the maximum investment period). The line 1 then

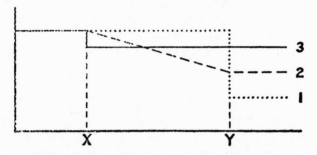

represents the income stream of the capitalist who goes on spending during the transition period XY as much as he did before, and thereby increases his capital in money terms, line 2 that of the capitalist who gradually increases his consumption and keeps his capital in money terms constant, and line 3 the income stream of the capitalist who immediately raises his consumptive expenditure to the level at which it can be permanently maintained (*i.e.*, until some further change occurs), and thereby decreases the money value of his capital.

There is no difficulty in applying the same kind of analysis to the reverse case of an expected decrease of the return from capital, or to almost any other type of change that may be foreseen. If the shift of demand, instead of taking place from a less to a more capitalistic line of industry, takes the reverse direction and the rate of interest is therefore due to fall, then a similar choice arises. Either the capitalist will anticipate the fall in his income and reduce it immediately in order to avoid, by an increase of his capital in monetary terms, the full force of the later reduction which would otherwise be inevitable (case 3). Or he will only gradually reduce it as his gross receipts from capital fall (case 2). Or he will maintain his expenditure until the change actually takes place, and so reduce even the money value of his capital, from which henceforth he will draw a smaller percentage return (case 1).

Action of the type 3, which I suggest in both cases comes nearest to what is really aimed at by capital accounting, but does not imply the maintenance of any dimension of capital as such, means in other words that the capitalist treats his gross receipts during the transition period as a terminable annuity of which he wants to consume no more than such a constant amount, that the sinking fund accumulated at the end of the period will secure him the same income in perpetuity. It is such action, which in my opinion best fulfils the purpose for which it is commonly desired to keep capital intact, from the point of view of the individual capitalist. It remains now to show what such action implies in the case of other types of changes, and what will be the effect of such action on the part of the capitalists on other incomes.

There is little more to be said about the effects of changes in the supply of factors, or—what is fundamentally the same thing—changes in technology. Since even an initial change in consumers' demand brings about changes in the relative scarcity of the different factors, there is really here no new problem beyond those already discussed. The anticipation of the forthcoming change will require the same kind of decision, and if the capitalist wants to keep his income stream constant after the impending change becomes known, he will have to redivide his changed gross receipts on the same principles as shown before. If, for instance, the supply of a factor of production is expected to decrease, or the production of a commodity in some other way to become more difficult,[1] or if on the other hand the discovery of new natural resources, or the invention of a new process facilitates the production of a commodity, this will again, as soon as the impending change becomes known, affect the decisions of the capital owners in a double way : it will affect the magnitude of the gross receipts from capital by way of the changes in the prices of the other factors that will occur in consequence of the adjustments to the expected change, and it will affect the return to be expected from the reinvestment of capital. The decision of the capitalist will accordingly depend in the same way on the effect of the change on the relative productivity of capital and the other factors, as was true in the former case. If the capitalist acts on the principle we have described as being most in accordance with what is the most obvious purpose of " maintaining capital intact," he

[1] Negative inventions, although apparently an absurd idea, are unfortunately by no means impossible. Losses of knowledge already possessed do occur, particularly in the field of economics, and the most glaring instance of this sort is, of course, the recrudescence of protectionism with its erection of negative railroads, to use Bastiat's very appropriate phrase.

will tend to let the money value of his capital decrease when in the future it promises to give a greater percentage return, because he will anticipate that greater future return ; and he will attempt to increase the money value of his capital by reducing his expenditure immediately when he expects in the future a lower percentage return.

While in this way the capitalist will minimise the fluctuations of his own income, his action will rather tend to accentuate the effect of the change on other incomes. At least, if instead of acting in this way he would try to keep the money value of his capital constant (and still more if he acted according to the third alternative—case 1—*i.e.*, if he kept his consumption constant until the expected change actually occurred), the incomes of the other factors would have to change to a much smaller degree than in the case where he aims at keeping the income from his capital constant. In the case where the marginal productivity of labour tends to fall and that of capital to rise, wages would have to fall less if the capitalists kept at least the money value of their capital constant and less still if they increased it. And in the reverse case wages would rise less if instead of maintaining or even raising the money value of their capital, capitalists allowed it to decrease. But there is little reason to assume that they will act in this way. Even where the capitalists do not want to keep their income constant under all circumstances but where, as will probably be the case to some extent, every increase of their expected income will induce them to plan for a gradually increasing consumption, *i.e.*, to save, and perhaps an expected decrease in their income will in the same way induce them to plan for a decreasing consumption, *i.e.*, to dissave, this is not very likely to result in a maintenance of the monetary value of capital (*i.e.*, to make their action similar to case 2 above). One would have to assume a very peculiar shape of the indifference curves expressing the " willingness to save " of the capitalists in order to obtain such a result.

5.   *Obsolescence and anticipated risks.* There remain two special cases to be considered before we abandon the assumption of correct foresight on the part of the capitalists. The first is obsolescence, as distinguished from wear and tear, as a cause of destruction of existing capital values. Although at first it may appear otherwise, this is a phenomenon which will occur even with perfect foresight. The second case on the other hand is somewhat intermediate between that of correct and incorrect foresight ; it is the case where the probability of the occurrence of certain changes is correctly and equally foreseen and estimated by all members of the society.   Since this case also raises the problem of obsolescence, it is convenient to treat the two cases together.

The first case would hardly require much discussion if Professor Pigou had not originally excluded obsolescence from the capital losses which have to be made up by new investment if capital is to be maintained intact. Obsolescence in this sense occurs everywhere where the usefulness of any piece of real capital diminishes faster than it decays in a physical sense. There can be no doubt that many investments in actual life are made with complete awareness of the fact that the period, during which the instrument concerned will be useful, will be much shorter than its possible physical duration. In the case of most very durable constructions like the permanent way of a railroad, the prospective " economic life " ought to be regarded as considerably shorter than the possible " physical life." In many cases it lies in the very nature of the product that it must be made almost infinitely durable, although it is only needed for a very transient purpose. It is impossible to adjust the durability of a machine to the short period during which it may be needed, and in many other cases the strength needed from a construction while it is used necessitates it being made in a form which will last much longer than the period during which it is needed.

In all these cases it is known beforehand that the stream of receipts to be obtained from the investment is limited, not only to the period for which the good will last physically, but for the shorter period during which it can be used. The capitalist who aims at a constant income stream will have to take this into account in deciding about the division of his gross receipts between consumption and amortisation. He will again have to treat the gross receipts as a terminable annuity, and to consume no more than such an amount that the sinking fund accumulated at the end of the period will give him in the form of a perpetual income. This means that he will have to put aside amounts proportional, not to the physical wear and tear, but to the decrease in the value of the investment.

If, instead of acting in this way, he would, as Professor Pigou suggests, at the end of every accounting period put aside out of his gross receipts only such a part of the value of the instrument as is proportional to the physical deterioration that has taken place during the period, this would clearly mean that he would consume considerably more than he could expect to derive from the much smaller sinking fund accumulated when the instrument ceases to be useful.

The significance of such a decision on the part of the capitalist becomes particularly clear if we consider the case where the capitalist has to choose between two investments of equal cost, both represented by equally durable instruments, but one of the kind that is expected to remain useful so long as it lasts physically, while the other serves a very transient purpose. Under what conditions will he consider the two investments as equally attractive ? The first answer is, of course, if they promise him the same permanent income. But under what conditions do they promise him the same permanent income ? If the gross receipts from the investments while they flow were in both cases equal and just sufficient to provide the same income *plus* an allowance for depreciation proportional to the physical deterioration, the effect would clearly be that in the case where the instrument ceases to be useful long before it has worn out physically, only a fraction of the sum originally invested would have been recovered which would bring only a much lower income in the future. To decide for this alternative would mean that an income stream which starts at a given magnitude but decreases later on is treated as equal to an income stream which is permanently kept at the initial magnitude of the former. In order that investment in the instrument of only transitory usefulness may appear equally attractive as that of lasting usefulness, it would be necessary that, while the former remains in use, it would produce gross returns sufficiently large to allow for full amortisation of its original value. In other words, only if the expected returns cover, in addition to the same income, not only depreciation in the narrower sense but also obsolescence, can the two investments be regarded as equally attractive.

Thus, to neglect obsolescence, in deciding about the investments to be chosen, would in the same way frustrate the endeavour to keep the income stream at any definite level, as would a neglect of depreciation proper. In fact, from a purely economic point of view, there is no real difference between depreciation and obsolescence. Whether an instrument ceases to be useful because of physical decay, or for any other reason, makes no difference to the capitalist, when he has to decide whether it is worth while to invest in it or not.

That there could exist any doubt whatever about this point is probably due to the fact that, while the case where it is definitely foreseen that an instrument will become obsolescent at a certain date is by no means rare, it is not the case of which we think in the first instance when we speak of obsolescence. Of much greater practical importance than this case, where an instrument has for technical reasons to be made more durable than is really needed, is the case where it has been given a greater durability than turns out ultimately to have been necessary, because the period during which it would be needed was not known for certain. In so far as the effects of completely unforeseen and unforeseeable changes are here concerned, we shall consider them only in the following section of this paper. But, as has already been mentioned, there is an intermediate class between this case and that of complete foresight, the case where a definite probability exists and is generally known that a change will occur. And this case, as will be shown, is fundamentally similar to that just discussed, in the sense that here, too, the anticipated risk of obsolescence has to be taken into account if capital is to be maintained intact.

The capitalist who considers a number of different investment opportunities will usually find that they promise different returns with different degrees of probability. And while the degree of certainty with which he will be able to predict returns may be fairly high in so far as the immediate future is concerned, uncertainty will generally be much greater as regards the period during which he may hope to receive these or any returns. But while he will be unable to predict with certainty the periods during which he may expect returns in the different cases, he will have fairly definite ideas about the different degrees of probability that they will give returns for longer or shorter periods. In his choice between different investment opportunities, these estimates of the probable periods after which they will cease to give returns will play an important role. He will evidently consider an investment, where the risk, that it will soon cease to give any returns, is greater than in other cases, only if the gross returns are such that he can expect to amortise the capital sunk in it during a correspondingly shorter period. Only when he distributes his capital in such a way between the different investment opportunities, that the gross returns cover the probable rate of obsolescence, can he hope to obtain a constant income stream. If he acts in this way, and if his estimates of the probabilities were correct, even if in none of the individual cases he should have guessed quite correctly, his losses are likely to be balanced, so that on the whole he will succeed in maintaining his income stream constant. This presupposes that his investments are sufficiently numerous and diverse to make such compensation possible, and that in the cases where he makes unexpected profits, *i.e.*, where the investment continues to bring returns after its original value has been fully amortised, he does not treat these profits as net income, but he uses them to offset the losses suffered from other investments. Where the investments of the individual capitalists are not sufficiently numerous and diverse to make such internal compensation possible, the same results will follow for the capitalists as a class, provided again that those who make profit do not consume them but use them or at least the greater part of them for new investment. Is there any reason to expect that in this case the capitalist, following the general principle we have regarded as normal, will behave in such a way? This brings us to the general question of how the capitalists will react on an entirely unforeseen change.

6. *The reaction of the capitalist on unforeseen changes.* The changes whose effects we have now to study differ from those considered in the earlier parts of this paper by the fact that they are not foreseen but become known only when they actually occur (or at least some time after the investment affected by them has irrevocably been made). That is, we abandon at this point the assumption of more or less complete foresight on the part of the capitalist, and ask how he will have to act when an unexpected change affects the

returns from an investment, to which he has already committed himself, if he wants to keep his income stream from that moment onwards constant.

The owner of any piece of real capital, who finds that in consequence of such an unforeseen change the gross returns which he may expect during the remaining " life " of that instrument will be either greater or smaller than he had anticipated, will have to choose between the same main types of action as those discussed in connection with a foreseen change. If we consider only the case where, in consequence of the change his gross receipts have decreased, he may in the first instance consume, during the remaining " life " of his investment as much as before (if the gross receipts are still as great as the amount he used to consume) and reduce only his depreciation allowance. The effect of this would be that when the returns from the investment cease he will only have accumulated a sinking fund considerably smaller than what would be necessary to give him an income equal to that enjoyed up to that moment. Or, in other words, he would have maintained his consumption after the change has occurred at the pre-existing level at the expense of an inevitable later reduction of his consumption, a reduction which would clearly have to be greater than if he had immediately reduced his consumption to a level at which it could be permanently maintained. To act in the latter way, *i.e.*, again to treat the gross receipts to be expected during the remaining life of the investment as a terminable annuity, whose capital value is to be maintained constant, would evidently be the only course of action consistent with the aim of a constant income stream. The third possibility would be to continue, after the change has occurred, so far as possible the same allowances for depreciation and to reduce consumption to what remains beyond this, if anything does remain. In this way it would be possible in many cases to recover the full capital value originally invested. But could this properly be regarded as maintaining the capital constant ? It would mean that the owner would have to reduce consumption for a period below the level at which it could be permanently maintained in order to increase it later above that level. It seems that this would have to be regarded in every sense as new saving, saving it is true to make up for a loss, but for a loss which has already occurred. This loss was irrevocably incurred when the investment was made in ignorance of the impending change.

The same applies, *mutatis mutandis*, to the case of profits due to an unexpected change. If, after a change which has increased the gross returns from his investment, the owner wants to keep his income permanently at the same higher level, this means that he must only consume so much of the gain as to leave an amount which, reinvested at the current rate of interest, would give him the same additional income in perpetuity. If, for instance, his additional receipts after the change are £210, and the rate at which he can reinvest is 5 per cent, he must only consume £10, and invest the remaining £200, which at 5 per cent will give him the same returns in every future year. Such " windfall profits " are, therefore, not income in the sense that their consumption is compatible with maintaining capital intact. Also consumption need not be reduced by the amount of " windfall losses " in order to maintain capital intact. In both cases only the current interest on the (positive or negative) capital gain ought to be counted as income.

This principle applies, whether the change in question was completely foreseen, or whether it is a change, the probability of whose occurrence was anticipated, but which does not occur at the moment that was regarded as most probable. The difference between the two cases is that where the probability of the occurrence of the change was correctly anticipated, deviations of the individual cases from what was regarded as most probable are likely to balance in their effect, so that capitalists as a whole will succeed in keeping their income stream constant. But, where the changes were completely unforeseen, there is no reason to expect that gains and losses will balance in this way, so that at least total incomes from capital would remain constant. It is much more likely that in such a case, if the capitalists behave as described, it will have the effect of either permanently decreasing or permanently increasing the income from capital.

Of the different types of changes which would have to be considered in the exhaustive discussion we may confine ourselves here to that of an invention, which is in many ways the most interesting. The application to the case of a shift in demand between different types of consumers' goods, or of changes in the supply of factors, will present no difficulty. In so far as the invention is concerned, two kinds of effects have to be considered ; on the one hand the possibility of a loss of capital invested in plant that is made obsolete by the invention, and on the other hand, the possible gains on plants and stock which, at least during a transition period, may bring higher returns than was expected. Although there is some reason to suppose that any unexpected change is much more likely to lead to considerable capital losses than to capital gains, it is not impossible that in the individual case the gains may be greater than the losses.

The conditions, which must be given, in order that it may be advantageous to introduce newly invented machinery for the production of a commodity, which up to the present has been produced by a different still existing plant, are too well known to need more than a short restatement.[1] In order that the invention should lead to the complete abandonment of the old machinery, it would be necessary that it should reduce the total cost of production below the prime cost of running the old plant (or, quite exactly, to such a figure that the difference between it and the prime cost is lower than the return to be expected from the investment of the scrap value of the old plant). In this case the capital value of the old plant would be completely destroyed (or reduced to the scrap value of the plant). Much more frequently will it be the case that, while the new invention does not result in a sufficient lowering of cost to drive the old plant out of business altogether, it will make an increase of sales at the reduced price possible. In this case only the additional output will be produced by the new process, and the value of the old plant will be reduced to a figure corresponding to the capitalised value of the lower surplus over running costs, which is

---

[1] Cf. Pigou, *Economics of Welfare*, 4th Ed., p. 188, Robbins, *An Essay on the Nature and Significance of Economic Science*, 1932, pp. 50 *et seq.*, and my inaugural address " On the Trend of Economic Thinking," *Economica*, May, 1933.

henceforward to be expected. In all these cases capital losses will occur, which may be further increased by a rise in the rate of interest, which may be the general effect of the increased demand for capital caused by the new invention. In so far as such a rise in the rate of interest takes place, the losses in capital values caused thereby are not inconsistent with maintaining capital (*i.e.*, income from capital) constant in our sense.

Capital gains will occur in consequence of an invention—apart from the increases in capital values of natural resources, like mineral deposits and other non-reproduceable factors—mainly during such transition periods until it is possible to increase the supply of particular instruments, which are now also required in the newly invented process. If, *e.g.*, the new machinery required can be produced only in a particular plant, which before was expected to be used up only very slowly over a long period, and if it takes a long time to erect an additional plant of the same sort, the owner of the existing plants will clearly be able to make considerable and unexpected profits during the interval. Since these profits will be of a temporary character, he ought not to regard them as ordinary income, but to reinvest so much of it as will secure him in perpetuity an additional income equal to that which he actually consumes during the transition period.[1]

---

[1] It is not possible here to enter into a discussion of the distinction between capital-saving and labour-saving inventions. But it should be clear that at least the older concept of capital-saving inventions which was based on the idea that capital which in the past was used in the industry affected by the invention will in consequence become available for use elsewhere, assumed a kind of capital maintenance which will not occur in the real world. The part of the capital embodied in the now antiquated machinery will be lost at the same time as it becomes " superfluous."

7. The impossibility of an objective standard with different degrees of foresight. So far the criterion, for what is to be understood as maintaining capital intact on the part of the individual entrepreneur or capitalist, is purely subjective, because it depends on the extent to which the individual capitalist foresees the future. Entirely different actions by two capitalists who hold different views on the future, but who are otherwise in exactly the same position, may satisfy our criterion. Both may, in the light of their different knowledge, do their best to obtain a constant income stream, and yet both will probably fail, earlier or later, and in different degrees. Are we to say that neither has been maintaining his capital, and ought we to reserve this term to the case of action with perfect foresight ? In a world where very imperfect foresight is the rule this would clearly lead to absurd results. We should not only have to say that nobody ever succeeds in maintaining his capital intact—which in a sense of course would be true—but we should also be prevented from using this concept of maintaining capital intact as a description of the actual behaviour of the entrepreneurs, who want neither to decrease nor to increase their income from their possessions. Taking into account the fact that human foresight is of necessity very imperfect, and that all economic activity must be based on anticipations, which will partly prove incorrect, it would still seem desirable to find a criterion which would enable us to distinguish between losses—or rather missed opportunities of faster improvement— which are unavoidable in view of the unpredictability of the change, and capital losses due to what appear to be avoidable mistakes.

At first one might feel inclined to base the definition of what is to be regarded as adequate maintenance of capital on such a degree of foresight as the intelligent capitalist can reasonably be expected to possess. But closer examination of the problem soon reveals that any attempt to find an objective test of what can be regarded as maintenance of capital, short of the case of absolute foresight, must necessarily fail. It seems common sense to say that if an entrepreneur expects a change in taste, *e.g.*, because he hopes to interest the public in a novelty, but is disappointed in his expectations, and loses the capital invested in the venture, this is a loss of capital which must be made up out of new savings, if capital is to be kept intact. If this did not happen, and similar failures were frequently repeated, the capital available for the production of things which people want would be considerably reduced by conversion into equipment for making things which nobody wants. On the other hand, the loss of capital due to an unforeseen change in taste seems merely the incidental and unavoidable concomitant of a process leading to what is now a preferred income. Yet if entrepreneurs had correctly anticipated the change—and some entrepreneurs may have done so—the wants of the public would have been supplied even better. Is, therefore, the loss of the entrepreneurs, who did not foresee correctly, to be counted as a capital loss to be deducted from gross output? and does it already mean that they might have foreseen the change if a single happy speculator chanced to do so, who, according to all reasonable expectations should have proved to be a waster of capital?

It is not possible to base the distinction here on the

concept of a change, and to say that to invest in anticipation of a change which does not occur is wasting
capital, while to invest in the mistaken assumption
that things will remain as they are is only a cause of
unavoidable loss. In the first instance, it is by no
means evident what is to be regarded as a change. If
a temporary change is mistakenly considered as permanent, or if the expectation that the seasonal fluctuations
of the past will be repeated is disappointed, are these
to be regarded as mistaken expectations of a change, or
as a mistaken expectation that things will remain
constant? Clearly in economic life, and outside of a
fictitious stationary state, the concept of a change
itself has frequently no meaning except in the sense of
a change relative to expectations. In the second
place, and even more important, an approximately
correct anticipation of the majority of " changes "
in the usual sense is an indispensable condition of that
degree of progress which is observed in actual life.
One need only consider for a moment what would
happen if entrepreneurs always acted as if things would
remain forever as they are at present, and changed
their plans only after a change in demand (or some other
change) had actually occurred, in order to see what
would necessarily be the effect on general productivity.
Every change would mean an enormous loss, or rather,
the adaptation of production to the change would
become so expensive (not because the loss on existing
investment would have to be counted as cost, but
because the " free capital " required for the new
production would be so scarce) as to make it in many
cases impossible. How rich, on the other hand, should

we now be if all past changes had been correctly foreseen from the beginning of things !

All this means simply that the mobility of capital, the degree to which it can be maintained in a changing world, will depend on the foresight of the entrepreneurs and capitalists. If this is a commonplace, it is at least a commonplace to which far too little regard is paid in usual reasoning. It means nothing less than that the amount of capital available at any moment in a dynamic society depends much more on the degree of foresight of the entrepreneurs than on current saving or on " time preference." This is simply a corollary to the equally obvious and neglected fact that " capital " is not a factor, the quantity of which is given independently of human action even in the comparatively short run. How great a contribution to the possibility of satisfying human wants a given stock of capital goods will still represent some time later, will depend largely on how correctly the entrepreneurs foresee the situation at this moment. Their anticipations in this respect are quite as important a " datum " for the explanation of the dynamic process as the " stock of capital," and the latter concept has in fact little meaning without the former. As an enumeration of individual capital goods existing at the beginning, the " stock of capital " is, of course, an important datum, but the form in which this capital will still exist some time afterwards, and how much of it will still exist, depends mainly on the foresight of the entrepreneurs and capitalists. It would probably be no exaggeration to say that to maintain his capital so as to receive the greatest lasting return, is the main function of the capitalist-entrepreneur.[1] But not only is in this sense the size of the productive equipment of society dependent on the success of the entrepreneur, it is also dependent in a world of uncertainty on his capitalising capital gains (" windfall profits "). It should be recognised that much of the new formation of capital equipment (which may, but need not, represent net additions to capital in the traditional terminology) does not arise out of savings proper, but out of those gains of individual capitalists which are part of the process of capital maintenance. This process will, as shown above, always involve unforeseen profits on the part of some and unforeseen losses on the part of other entrepreneurs, changes on capital account, which are part of an ever-proceeding process of redistribution of wealth, not to be confused with the distribution of income. The entrepreneur who finds that a risky undertaking succeeds, and who for a time makes extraordinary profits because he has restricted the amount of investment so as to give him in case of success a margin of profit over cost which is proportionate to the risk, will not be justified if he regards the whole profit as income. If he aims at a constant income stream from his investment, he will have to reinvest such part of his profits as will be sufficient to give him an income equal to the part he has consumed, when the rate of profit in what has now proved to be a successful line of business falls to normal.[2] It

[1] In this connection it is hardly possible to draw a sharp distinction between the entrepreneur and capitalist.

[2] It is, of course, possible that he regards himself as so much more clever than his competitors that he will count on being able to make permanently supernormal profits of this sort. To this extent he would be quite justified in regarding them as income.

is in such a way that, in case of changes in demand
or technical progress, etc., capital is newly formed
without new saving in place of that which is lost elsewhere. There is, of course, no reason to assume that
the capital lost and that which is newly formed will
correspond in any quantitative sense ; and it is exactly
for this reason that the usual concept of a net change
in capital, which is supposed to correspond in some way
to saving, is of little value. There has in this case been
no abstention from consumption which could have
been maintained at that level. If anybody can be said
to have refrained from consumption which would be
compatible with enjoying the same income permanently,
it is not the entrepreneurs, but rather the consumers
who for a time had to pay a price in excess of the cost
which the production of the commodity entails after
it has proved an assured success. But this " saving " is,
of course, neither voluntary nor does it represent an
abstention from consumption, which could have
been regarded as permanently possible so long as the
outcome of the venture was uncertain. It can hardly
be questioned that in the actual world a great deal
of the equipment which is made necessary by some
change is financed out of these temporary differences
between cost and price. But it may appear somewhat
paradoxical that where it can be provided in this way
this ought not to be classed as saving but as a capital
gain, a kind of transfer of capital which means that
not only new capital is formed in place of that lost
elsewhere, but that it is formed exactly where it is
most needed, and in the hands of those most qualified
to use it ; this follows, however, necessarily from the
consistent use of the definition of maintaining capital

and saving, which we have adopted. It will be shown in the next section that this use of the terms proves convenient in other directions also.

8. "*Saving*" *and* "*Investing.*" The upshot of the discussions of the last sections is that if changes in the data occur (such as new inventions, shifts in consumers' demand or changes in the supply of factors), the amount of capital (conceived as a multiple of the income of a given period, or—what amounts to the same thing—the result of a certain " average " waiting period, or in any other conceivable quantitative sense), which is available and required to maintain income from then onwards at a constant level, will change also, and that in consequence there is no reason to expect that any of the conceivable dimensions of capital will remain constant. It remains true, of course, that *ceteris paribus* it is necessary to maintain or replenish a reservoir of goods of a constant size, in order to maintain a given output. But when conditions change so as to make a smaller or larger reservoir necessary for the same purpose, its contents will tend to change automatically in such a way as to preserve income constant from the moment when the change becomes known. The fact that an impending change is likely to become known to different people at different times will lead to capital gains and capital losses of individuals, with the effect that persons who have shown the greatest foresight will command the greatest amount of resources. But in a world of imperfect foresight not only the size of the capital stock, but also the income derived from it will inevitably be subject to unintended and unpredictable changes which depend on the extent and distribution of foresight, and there

will be no possibility of distinguishing any particular movement of these magnitudes as normal.

These conclusions have rather far-reaching consequences with respect to the much used, or much abused, concepts of saving and investing. If the stock of capital required to keep income from any moment onwards constant cannot in any sense be defined as a constant magnitude, it becomes also impossible to state that any sacrifices of present income in order to increase future income (or the reverse) must lead to any net changes in the amount of capital. Saving and investment in the ordinary meaning of the terms are, of course, one of the causes, but by no means the only cause, which affect the magnitude of capital (in any conceivable quantitative sense), and the changes in the size of the capital stock cannot therefore be regarded as indications of what sacrifices of present income have been or are being made in the interest of future income. This idea, appropriately enough for the analysis of the effects of a change under otherwise stationary conditions, must be completely abandoned in the analysis of a dynamic process. If we want to retain the connection between the ideas of saving and investment, and that of a sacrifice of potential present income in the interest of future income (and it will be shown that it is this concept which is of importance in the connection in which those terms are commonly used), we cannot determine the size of either saving or investment by any references to changes in the quantity of capital. And with the abandonment of this basis of the distinction, there will, of course, have to fall the habitual practice of economists of separating out such part of general investment activity as happens to leave the capital stock in some sense constant, as something different from activities which add to it, a distinction which has no relationship to anything in the real world.[1]

To deny that the usual distinctions between new and merely renewed investment, and between new savings out of net income and merely maintained savings, as distinctions based on the idea of quantitative increases or decreases of capital, have any definite meaning, is not to deny that they aim at a distinction of real importance. There can be no doubt that the decision of the consumers as to the distribution of consumption over time are something separate from the decisions of the entrepreneur-capitalist as regards what quantities of consumers' goods to provide for different moments of time, and that the two sets of decisions may or may not coincide. What I do want to deny is only that the correspondence or non-correspondence between these two sets of conditions can be adequately expressed in terms of a quantitative correspondence between (net) saving and (net) investment. But if this distinction is not to be formulated in this particular way, what are we to put in its place? In general terms the answer is not difficult. If we must no longer speak in terms of absolute increases and decreases of capital we must attempt a more direct comparison of the time distribution of income. Capital accounting, as has

---

[1] The same applies, of course, in an even stronger degree to the assumption implied in this distinction that the activities which lead to such net increases of capital are in any way subject to a different set of determining influences from those which lead to a mere quantitative maintenance. This should always have been obvious from the mere fact that when additions in this sense are being made (*i.e.*, if capital increases in the usual terminology) this will always affect the concrete form of the new capital goods by which the old ones are replaced.

been mentioned before, is itself only an abbreviated method of effecting this comparison in an indirect way, and when this indirect method fails it is only natural to go back to its *rationale*, and to carry out the comparison explicitly. Instead of comparing them each with the supposed standard case of capital remaining " constant," and so arriving at the concepts of net saving (net income *minus* consumption) and net investment, and then to juxtapose these derived concepts, we shall have to compare directly the intentions of the consumers and the intentions of the producers with regard to the income stream they want to consume and produce respectively.

The question, then, is essentially whether the demand for consumers' goods tends to keep ahead of, to coincide with, or to fall behind the output of consumers' goods irrespective of whether either of the two magnitudes is increasing, remaining constant or decreasing in an absolute sense. But in order to give this question a clear meaning we have yet to settle in terms of what are the demand for and the supply of consumers' goods to be measured, in order to establish whether they coincide or whether the one exceeds the other. In a sense, of course, demand and supply are always equal, or made equal by the pricing process, and to speak of their relative magnitudes presupposes some unit in terms of which their magnitude is measured independently of the prices formed on the market.

Consider first the decision of the " savers," or the body of consumers as a whole. What we can assume of them is, not that they will under all conditions aim at an income stream of a particular shape, but that if they are offered a present income of a given magnitude, *plus* the sources of a future income of a certain magnitude, they will attach certain relative values to these incomes. For every such combination of a given present income and the sources of a certain future income we must assume these relative valuations to be determined.

If the relative value consumers attach to the sources of future income, compared with present values, should be higher (or lower) than the cost (in terms of present income) of reproducing new sources of future income of the same magnitude, more (or less) such sources will be produced. And assuming that the relative valuations of the consumers do not change abruptly—which is least to be expected when in each successive period the available income is equal to that for which they have planned—then production will tend to provide in each successive period such amounts of present income and sources of future income, that their relative cost (in terms of each other) will approximately correspond to the relative values attached to them by the consumers. But if for some reason—say because additional money has become available for investment purposes—the price of the sources of future income have been raised out of correspondence with the valuation of consumers, more sources of future income and less current income will be provided for the next period than consumers will be then willing to take at prices corresponding to their relative cost. Consumers will find that they get less current real income, and in consequence will attach a greater value to it compared with the sources of future income—investment will have exceeded saving in the usual terminology.

Under the assumption of otherwise constant conditions (*i.e.*, unchanged knowledge, taste, etc.) this process can be described in the familiar way in terms of changes of the investment period, to which correspond changes in the quantity of capital (in terms of income of a period). We would say that, by increasing the waiting period and thereby accumulating more capital, producers have caused a temporary gap in the income stream which leads to a relative rise in the prices of consumers' goods. But as soon as we drop this *ceteris paribus* assumption this is no longer true. The correspondence between the value attached to the sources of future income and their cost is then no longer dependent on the cost of reproducing the same amount of capital, which under changed conditions will make it possible to produce the same future income.

Additional investment, in the sense that total output is reduced for a time in order to increase it at a later date, may take place, although at the same time the quantity of capital is reduced (and the " period of production " shortened).[1] Breaks in the even flow of consumers' goods, which make corresponding changes in the attitude of the consumers necessary if disturbances are to be avoided will only occur when that quantity of capital is not maintained which under the conditions prevailing at any moment is required to provide such a constant flow.

The correspondence between the supply of current consumers' goods and the demand for them, which is what has been aimed at by the saving-investment

[1] This does not, of course, affect the fundamental proposition that the additional saving is required to make an extension of the process of production possible compared with the time dimension that would be possible without this saving.

equations, can only be stated adequately if we measure both supply and demand in terms of the alternatives open to consumers and producers under the circumstances existing at the moment.[1] To do this it seems necessary to abandon entirely the concepts of saving and investment as referring to something beyond and outside the normal process of maintaining capital quantitatively intact, and to substitute an analysis on the lines suggested, which does not try to separate " old " and " new " investment, and " new " and " maintained " saving as distinguishable phenomena. Or, if we want to retain the familiar terms and to use them without any reference to changes in the quantity of capital, we might say that " savings " correspond to " investment " when the value of the existing capital goods (in terms of consumers' goods) is such that it becomes profitable to replace them by the capital goods that are required to produce the income in the expectation of which people have decided currently to consume as much as they actually do. I believe that some theories, which used to be stated in terms of net saving and net investment, can be restated in terms of these concepts, and I have tried to sketch

---

[1] All this might apparently have been explained in simpler fashion by comparing the cost of the output of consumers' goods coming on the market during a given period with the expenditure on this output (or by comparing the share of all factors of production which have contributed to the output of a given period with the share of their income which is spent on the output), if it were not for the fact that the concept of cost (and, of course, income) is itself dependent on the concept of maintaining capital intact. This way of stating the relation would be adequate only if we count the cost (in terms of present consumption) which is required, *not* to keep capital intact in some quantitative sense, but to provide sources of so much future income as consumers want to buy at prices covering cost.

such a reformulation of my own views in another place.[1] But I am rather doubtful whether the same is possible with some other theories which seem more dependent on the concepts of saving and investing as absolute magnitudes.

All this is, of course, no reason for not using the concepts of absolute increases or decreases of capital under any circumstances. In the discussion of comparatively long-term changes it may sometimes be quite innocuous. And in the discussion of short-run changes it would be equally legitimate to speak of causes, which *ceteris paribus* would lead to increases or decreases of capital. But we must be very careful not to assume that they actually do, and not to base any distinctions on supposed net changes in the quantity of capital which do not actually take place. Particularly the phenomenon of the trade cycle is probably largely concerned with changes within that region of indeterminateness between clear increases and clear decreases of capital, inside which the concept of an absolute change has no meaning. But it remains probably true that net accumulations and decumulations of capital in the usual sense will present similar phenomena as booms and depressions—at least when real accumulation proceeds faster and real decumulation proceeds slower than saving and dissaving.[2]

[1] Cf. " Price Expectations, Monetary Disturbances and Malinvestments " now reprinted as the fourth essay in this volume, see below p. 135 *et seq.*

[2] Ricardo seems to have seen clearly the difficulties which exist in this connection when he wrote : " The distress which proceeds from a revulsion of trade is often mistaken for that which accompanies a diminution of the national capital and a retrograde state of society ; and it would perhaps be difficult to point out any marks by which they may be accurately distinguished." *Principles*, Ch. xix, *Works*, Edition McCulloch, p. 160.

9. *Capital accounting and monetary policy*. This discussion of the problems connected with the concept of the maintenance of capital has by no means been exhaustive. We have touched on many points which have not been cleared up, and there are many others equally important which have not even been mentioned. This is, however, unavoidable in an essay which treats what is in many respects one of the central problems of economic dynamics. But there is one further problem of great importance on which some remarks must be added in this concluding section.

Up to this point we have been largely concerned with an attempt to derive the appropriate action from the *rationale* of " maintaining capital intact," but we have said little about the effects of the actual practice of the entrepreneur, that " abbreviated method " which consists in regarding capital as a money fund of definite magnitude, and on which actual capital accounting is based. This practice is, of course, largely due, and partly justified, by the fact that the capital of the individual enterprise is to a great extent furnished in the form of money loans, and that in consequence the entrepreneur has in the first instance to provide for a repayment of the money loans.

It was also this practice of treating capital as a money fund which has given rise to the theoretical concept of capital as a quantitatively determined fund. But while the actual use of this concept in real life does not mean that we have to accept it as the basis of theoretical analysis, and does not relieve us from the duty of going back to the *rationale* of its use, the results of this theoretical investigation are little more than a starting point for a study of the effects of the actual practice.

A more exhaustive investigation would, therefore, have to proceed after this preliminary clearing up of the fundamental concepts to the main task of explaining what the effects are of the actual accounting methods used by capitalists, to what extent, and under what conditions, they fulfil their purpose, and when they fail. That there are cases where the rigid application of the money fund concept fails is, of course, generally recognised and to some extent taken account of in the distinction made between changes on income account and changes on capital account. It is also obvious that the results achieved by this method will be largely dependent on monetary policy. Of course, no monetary policy can make the money value of capital behave in such a way that a constant value will always correspond to a quantity of capital which will give the same real income, and that all attempts to increase the future output of consumers' goods at the expense of the present and vice versa will lead to corresponding changes in the money value of capital ; and in consequence a policy of the capitalist-entrepreneur which aims at nothing but this, will always err to a considerable extent, *i.e.*, will lead to positions where their distribution of resources between current consumption and the provision of future consumption is not in accord with consumers' preferences. But the degree to which capital accounting in terms of money will prove deceptive will depend on the particular monetary policy followed.

To realise these effects in different situations would require a fairly detailed analysis of a number of representative instances. It is only possible to discuss here in the most general way one case, probably the most important and the one which has received the greatest attention in recent discussion ; that of a continued increase in output due to " technical progress." Now, in spite of all the complications discussed before, it still remains true that *in any given situation* the value of capital required to provide an income stream at a certain constant or increasing rate will have to stand in a definite proportion to the value of current income. This proportion will change with any change in the relevant data, but where we have to deal with a development from moment to moment it is still approximately true to say that in order that the replacement of capital be sufficient to maintain the income stream at least at a constant rate its value should maintain a constant proportion to that of income. With the money value of capital being kept constant this will evidently only be true if the money value of aggregate income be kept constant also. Any policy which increases the money value of current income and particularly a policy which stabilises the average prices of consumers' goods and therefore raises the aggregate value of income in proportion as real income rises would mean that the money value of capital has to be raised in the same proportion and to be maintained at this increased value if sufficient provision for the replacement of this income is to be made. Any use of the nominal profits of the money value of capital so made for consumption purposes, as would follow from a policy of maintaining money values constant, would lead to insufficient replacement or a consumption of capital in the usual sense.

There can be no doubt that this sort of " paper profits " has played an enormous role not only during the great inflations, but also during all major booms— even if no rise in the absolute level of the prices of consumers' goods has taken place.   And even more important than the pseudo-profits computed by enterprises under such conditions are the gains on capital appreciation made on the Stock Exchange. Stock Exchange profits made during such periods of capital appreciation in terms of money, which do not correspond to any proportional increase of capital beyond the amount which is required to reproduce the equivalent of current income, are not income, and their use for consumption purposes must lead to a destruction of capital.[1] So long as the expansion of credit, which has caused this movement, continues at a sufficient rate, this tendency may be overcompensated and the money value of capital continue to grow.   But the monetary demand for consumers' goods fed out of such pseudo-profits will prove too large to permit of a main-tenance of capital at a proportional value without constant further expansion of credit. That the increas-ing money values of capital cannot be maintained without further inflation if the amount of appreciation is generally used for consumption purposes, is, of course, only another form of expressing the truism that capital values, which people in general try to convert into income, cannot be maintained beyond the time during which some outside cause operates in the direction of a further rise. But as soon as the cause of a further rise disappears the inherent tendency to

[1] It is in this way, and in this way only, that during a boom the Stock Exchange is likely to " absorb savings."

" realise " the nominal profits, *i.e.*, to convert part of the capital into income, will assert itself and lead to a fall even in the money value of capital.

But at this point we must stop. This final sketch of some of the conclusions that seem to arise was only meant to suggest some of the problems out of the wide field which opens up at the point where we left the main investigations. It seems that the approach to which it leads may ultimately help much to judge the significance of actual business practices, particularly the practices of joint stock companies, the different methods of financing and the Stock Exchange. The students of these fields have in the past had little enough help from the theory of capital. The ultimate clearing up of the issues raised in this article should go far to provide them with better tools.

PRICE EXPECTATIONS, MONETARY DISTURBANCES AND MALINVESTMENTS[1]

I

THE most characteristic feature of the work of our generation of economists is probably the general endeavour to apply the methods and results of the pure theory of equilibrium to the elucidation of more complicated " dynamic " phenomena. Perhaps one might have expected all generations of economists to have striven to approach nearer to reality by gradually relaxing the degree of abstraction of pure theory. Yet advance in this direction was not great during the fifty years preceding say 1920. The development of economics has not proceeded along the systematic lines of the textbook which advances step by step from the general to the particular. The answers to the pressing questions of real life could not wait till the slow progress of pure theory provided a scheme which would allow of immediate application in the more practical work.

---

[1] This essay reproduces the main argument of a lecture delivered on December 7th, 1933, in the *Sozialökonomisk Samfund* in Copenhagen and was first published (in German) in the *Nationalökonomisk Tidsskrift*, Vol. 73, No. 3, 1935, and later (in French) in the *Revue de Science Economique*, Liège, October, 1935.

It seems that as regards the attitude towards the applications of pure theory to the most complicated phenomena of economic dynamics, crises and industrial fluctuations, we can distinguish three main types. In many instances the men who most strongly felt the urgency of the problems existing in this field and attempted to solve them had little knowledge of the state of economic theory. This group includes, in addition to numberless cranks, several clear thinkers of rich experience to whom we are greatly indebted. A second group of men which is hardly less important consisted of scholars who, although well versed in current theoretical speculation, regarded it as of little use for the task in which they were mainly interested. Both groups have considerable achievements to their credit and I shall later have occasion to mention some important contributions from about 1850 onwards which we owe to them. It is by no means clear that this debt is smaller than that which we owe in this field to the third group, namely to those scholars who attempted—as it may appear to us, prematurely—to apply an over-simplified and defective theory to these complicated phenomena. Although their endeavour to justify in this way their concentration on pure theory and to demonstrate its usefulness was undoubtedly right, and although their instinct that only this path would ultimately lead to a really satisfactory explanation was right, the result of these early attempts, from the celebrated *Théorie des Débouchés* onwards, was frequently to press the problems into the strait-jacket of a scheme which did not really help to solve them.

II

It was only the modern development of equilibrium analysis together with the increasing awareness of the conditions and limitations of the applicability of the equilibrium concept which has taught us to recognise the nature of the problems existing in this field and which has indicated the paths towards their solution. And even if the different students of these problems proceed along different routes, it is probably true to-day to say that in all countries with a great theoretical tradition the efforts of the younger men in our subject is directed towards bridging the gulf between " statics " and " dynamics." To some the differences which exist here between different " schools " may appear very large. Yet whether the different individuals, in their zeal to advance, stress the deficiencies of the existing " static " theory more or less strongly appears to me to be based much more on differences of temperament than on differences in the aims or in the methods used. I believe that the great majority of the younger economists share the belief that the continuity of the development can be preserved and that only this will help us to reach our goal.

What we all seek is therefore not a jump into something entirely new and different but a development of our fundamental theoretical apparatus which will enable us to explain dynamic phenomena. Not very long ago I myself still believed that the best way to express this was to say that the theory of the trade cycle at which we were aiming ought to be organically superimposed upon the existing theory of equilibrium. I am now more inclined to say that general theory itself ought to be developed so as to enable us to use it directly in the explanation of particular industrial fluctuations. As has recently been shown very convincingly by Dr. Lutz,[1] our task is not to construct a separate theory of the trade cycle, that is of a construction of a detailed scheme which will fit all actual trade cycles, but rather a development of those sections of general theory which we need in the analysis of particular cycles—which often differ from one another very considerably.

A great part of this work will certainly consist in the elaboration of particular chapters of general theory, especially of the theory of capital and the theory of money, in the direction of a more careful analysis of the processes resulting from any change in the data. It is, however, the common peculiarity of all such attempts to make the theory more realistic that they soon bring us back to the fundamental problem of all economic theory, that is to the question of the significance of the concept of equilibrium and its relevance to the explanation of a process which takes place in time. There can be no doubt that here some of the formulations of the theory of equilibrium prove to be of little use and that not only their particular content but also the idea of equilibrium as such which they use will require a certain amount of revision.

That this concept of equilibrium has in the past not always had the same meaning and that this meaning has often not been very clear can hardly be denied. This is at least true of the application of the concept of equilibrium to the phenomena of a competitive

[1] F. Lutz, *Das Konjunkturproblem in der Nationalökonomie.* Jena, 1932.

society, while if applied to the economic activities of an isolated person or of a centrally directed communist system it probably has a definite meaning. While in this latter case we can legitimately speak of a necessary equilibrium between the decisions which a person will make at a given moment, it is much less clear in what sense we can apply the same concept to the actions of a great number of persons, whose successive reponses to the actions of their fellow-beings necessarily take place in time, and which can be represented as a timeless equilibrium relationship only by means of unrealistic special constructions.

Equilibrium analysis certainly needs, if we want to apply it to a changing competitive system, much more exact definitions of its basic assumptions than are commonly given. The realistic significance of the tendencies towards a state of equilibrium, traditionally described by pure theory, can be shown only when we know what the conditions are under which it is at least conceivable that a position of equilibrium will actually be reached.

The main difficulty of the traditional approach is its complete abstraction from time. A concept of equilibrium which essentially was applicable only to an economic system conceived as timeless could not be of great value. Fortunately in recent times there have been considerable changes on this very point. It has become clear that, instead of completely disregarding the time element, we must make very definite assumptions about the attitude of persons towards the future. The assumptions of this kind which are implied in the concept of equilibrium are essentially that everybody foresees the future correctly and that this foresight includes not only the changes in the objective data but also the behaviour of all the other people with whom he expects to perform economic transactions.[1]

It is not my intention to enter here more fully into these recent developments of equilibrium analysis and I hope what I have said will suffice to explain certain conclusions which I want to draw from them as to the study of dynamic phenomena. It appears to me that from this new angle it should at last become possible to give somewhat more definite meaning to certain concepts which most of us have been using somewhat loosely. I am thinking in particular of the statement frequently made that a whole economic system (or a particular price, as *e.g.*, the rate of interest) either is or is not in equilibrium.

It is evident that the various expectations on which different individuals base their decisions at a particular moment either will or will not be mutually compatible ; and that if these expectations are not compatible those of some people at least must be disappointed. It is probably clear also that expectations existing at a particular moment will to a large extent be based on prices existing at that moment and that we can conceive of constellations of such prices which will create expectations inevitably doomed to disappointment, and of other constellations which do not bear the germ of such disappointments and which create expectations which—at least if there are no unforeseen changes in external circumstances—may be in harmony with the

[1] Since the above was written I have further elaborated and partly revised this discussion of the relationship between equilibrium and foresight in a paper on " Economics and Knowledge," published in *Economica* for February, 1937.

actual course of events. This consideration appears to me to provide a useful starting point for further developments of the theory of industrial fluctuations.

III

Every explanation of economic crises must include the assumption that entrepreneurs have committed errors. But the mere fact that entrepreneurs do make errors can hardly be regarded as a sufficient explanation of crises. Erroneous dispositions which lead to losses all round will appear probable only if we can show why entrepreneurs should all simultaneously make mistakes in the same direction. The explanation that this is just due to a kind of psychological infection or that for any other reason most entrepreneurs should commit the same avoidable errors of judgment does not carry much conviction. It seems, however, more likely that they may all be equally misled by following guides or symptoms which as a rule prove reliable. Or, speaking more concretely, it may be that the prices existing when they made their decisions and on which they had to base their views about the future have created expectations which must necessarily be disappointed. In this case we might have to distinguish between what we may call justified errors, caused by the price system, and sheer errors about the course of external events. Although I have no time to discuss this further, I may mention that there is probably a close connection between this distinction and the traditional distinction between " endogenous " and " exogenous " theories of the trade cycle.

The most interesting case, for our present purpose, of such decisions of entrepreneurs where the outcome depends entirely on the correctness of the views *generally* held about future developments, is, of course, the case of investments in so far as these are affected by the situation of the capital market in general and not by the special position of particular industries. Here the same cause may bring about malinvestments not only in one or a few but in all industries at the same time. The success of almost any investment made for a considerable period of time will depend on the future development of the capital market and of the rate of interest. If at any moment people begin to add to the productive equipment this will as a rule represent only a part of a new process which will be completed only by further investments spread over a period of time ; and the first investment will therefore prove to have been successful only if the supply of capital makes the expected further developments at later dates possible. In general it is probably true to say that most investments are made in the expectation that the supply of capital will for some time continue at the present level. Or, in other words, entrepreneurs regard the present supply of capital and the present rate of interest as a symptom that approximately the same situation will continue to exist for some time. And it is only some such assumption that will justify the use of any additional capital to begin new round-about methods of production which, if they are to be completed, will require continued investment over a further period of time. (These further investments which are necessary if the present investments are going to be successful may be either investments by the same entrepreneurs who made the first investment, or—much more frequently—investments in the products produced by the first group by a second group of entrepreneurs.) If these expectations are to be realised it is necessary not that the supply of capital during the relevant period remains absolutely unchanged, but, as I have tried to show on another occasion,[1] that during no interval of time should it fall by more than has before been utilised to start new processes (as distinguished from continuing uncompleted ones).

Very large and unforeseen fluctuations of saving would therefore be sufficient to cause extensive losses on investments made during the period preceding them and therefore to create the characteristic situation of an economic crisis. The cause of such a crisis would be that entrepreneurs had mistakenly regarded a temporary increase in the supply of capital as permanent and acted in this expectation. The only reason why we cannot regard this as a sufficient explanation of economic crises as we know them is that experience provides no ground for assuming that such violent fluctuations in the rate of saving will occur otherwise than in consequence of crises. If it were not for the crises, which therefore we shall have to explain in a different way, the assumption of the entrepreneurs that the supply of saving will continue at about the present level for some time would probably prove to be justified. The decisions of the entrepreneurs as to

---

[1] Cf. the article on "Capital and Industrial Fluctuations," *Econometrica*, Vol. 2, No. 2, April, 1934 (now reprinted as appendix to the second edition of *Prices and Production*) where I have also somewhat more fully explained the distinction between complete and incomplete processes of production alluded to in the text.

the dates and quantities of consumers' goods for which they provide by their present investments would coincide with the intention of the consumers as to the parts of their incomes which they want to consume at the various dates.

IV

It is, of course, a well-known fact that the current supply of money-capital is not necessarily identical with the amount of current savings. All sorts of monetary disturbances, shortly described as changes in the quantity of money and changes in the velocity of circulation of money but in fact much more variegated in nature than these terms at first suggest, may change the supply of money capital independently of the supply of savings. This means, however, that entrepreneurs will often base their decisions about their investment plans on a symptom which in no way indicates even the current willingness of the consumers to save, and therefore provides no guide whatever for a forecast of how they will distribute their income in the future between consuming and saving. Entrepreneurs will make their decisions about the volume of their investments, *i.e.*, about the quantities of consumers' goods they will produce at various dates, as if the present distribution of monetary demand between consumers' goods and investments corresponded to the way in which the consumers divide their income between consuming and saving. The result of this must be that the proportion in which entrepreneurs will divide their resources between production for the near future

and production for the distant future will be different
from the proportion in which consumers' in general
want to divide their current income between current
consumption and provision for consumption at a
later date.

In such a situation there exists evidently a conflict
between the intentions of the consumers and the
intentions of entrepreneurs which earlier or later must
manifest itself and frustrate the expectations of at least
one of these two groups. The situation is certainly not
one of equilibrium in the sense defined before. A
condition of equilibrium would require that the intentions of the two groups are at least compatible. It
precludes a situation in which current prices, and particularly current rates of interest, create expectations
concerning the future behaviour of some members of
the society which are entirely unfounded. An equilibrium rate of interest would then be one which assured
correspondence between the intentions of the consumers and the intentions of the entrepreneurs. And
with a constant rate of saving this would be the rate
of interest arrived at on a market where the supply of
money capital was of exactly the same amount as
current savings.

If the supply of money capital is increased, by
monetary changes, beyond this amount, the result
will be that the rate of interest will be lowered below
the equilibrium rate and entrepreneurs will be induced
to devote a larger part of the existing resources to
production for the more distant future than corresponds
to the way in which consumers divide their income
between saving and current consumption. At the
time when the entrepreneurs make this decision the

consumers have no possibility of expressing their wishes with sufficient emphasis since their money incomes are as yet unchanged while the expansion of credit has increased the fund available for investment. The investment of these funds, however, must in the course of time increase total income by nearly the full amount of these funds, either because wages are raised in order to attract people away from producing consumers' goods towards producing capital goods, or because the funds are used to employ formerly unemployed workers. This will certainly tend to increase the intensity of the demand for consumers' goods—how far will depend on how consumers distribute their additional money income between consuming and saving.

The first point which we must keep in mind here is that this increase in aggregate money incomes cannot mean an increase of real incomes and is much more likely to mean a decrease of real incomes to many individual consumers. However great the amount of money at the disposal of the consumers, they can never consume more than the current supply of consumers' goods—and if the new investments have led to a diversion of already employed factors into longer processes of production, this must lead, to that extent, to an actual decrease of the current output of consumers' goods. The increase in the returns from the existing permanent resources in consequence of the new investments will not come until much later. But even when the first results of the new investments begin to come on the market, this increase in the output will amount to only a fraction of the additional incomes and, as will appear in a moment, it is this relation between the increase in incomes and the increase in the output of consumers' goods which is relevant to our problem.

There is little reason to assume that, in the circumstances we are considering, the share of the increased money incomes spent on current consumption will be diminished. The willingness to save on the part of the consumers will have been little affected by these changes ; and their capacity to save will, if anything, have decreased. Only in so far as redistributions of income have taken place during the whole process, favouring those more inclined to save at the expense of those less inclined to save, a certain increase in the proportion of the income actually saved may be expected. But whether the consumers divide their additional money income in the old proportion between current consumption and saving, or whether the proportion is slightly more favourable to saving, the increase in money incomes will in any case lead to an increase in the monetary demand for consumers' goods and therefore to an increase in the prices of consumers' goods.

This increased intensity of the demand for consumers' goods need have no unfavourable effect on investment activity so long as the funds available for investment purposes are sufficiently increased by further credit expansion to claim, in the face of the increasing competition from the consumers' goods industries, such increasing shares of the total available resources as are required to complete the new processes already under way. That this requires a continued expansion of credit proceeding at a progressive rate and that this, even apart from all legal or traditional obstacles, cannot be continued indefinitely, even if it were only because it would inevitably lead to a cumulative rise in prices which earlier or later would exceed any limit, is not difficult to see.[1] What is mainly of interest for our present purpose is, however, what will happen when the inevitable moment comes when the demand for consumers' goods begins to rise not only absolutely but also relatively to the funds available for investment.

v

We have now reached the point where the conflict between the intentions of the consumers and the intentions of the investors begins to manifest itself— the conflict caused by the distortion of the capital market by credit expansion. The entrepreneurs who have begun to increase their productive equipment in the expectation that the low rate of interest and the ample supply of money capital would enable them to continue and to utilise these investments under the same favourable conditions, find these expectations disappointed. The increase of the prices of all those factors of production that can be used also in the late stages of production will raise the costs of, and at the same time the rise in the rate of interest will decrease the demand for, the capital goods which they produce. And a considerable part of the newly created equipment designed to produce other capital goods will stand idle because the expected further investment in these other capital goods does not materialise.

[1] See in this connection my article in *Econometrica*, already quoted, particularly pp. 161 f.

This phenomenon of a scarcity of capital making it impossible to use the existing capital equipment appears to me the central point of the true explanation of crises ; and at the same time it is no doubt the one that rouses most objections and appears most improbable to the lay mind. That a scarcity of capital should lead to the existing capital goods remaining partly unused, that the abundance of capital goods should be a symptom of a shortage of capital, and that the cause of this should be not an insufficient but an excessive demand for consumers' goods, is apparently more than a theoretically untrained mind is readily persuaded to accept. Yet the truth of these apparent paradoxes appears to me to be established beyond doubt. Before I proceed to explain them further it is perhaps not inappropriate to show that some of the most experienced observers of the crises of the mid-nineteenth century had been constrained to accept them.

Their explanations of these crises were usually expressed in terms of an excessive conversion of circulating capital into fixed capital, induced by the creation of " fictitious capital,"[1] and leading in the end to a scarcity of " disposable " or " floating " capital which made a completion of many of the newly started ventures impossible. The author who mainly developed and popularised this doctrine in connection with the great railway booms and the following crises in the middle of the nineteenth century was the first editor of the *Economist*, James Wilson. It was later taken up by a group of Manchester economists and finally introduced into academic economics by Bonnamy Price in England

---

[1] On the origin of this term see now J. Viner, *Studies in the Theory of International Trade*, 1937, p. 196 note.

and Courcelle-Seneuil and V. Bonnet in France. And Yves Guyot even summed up the fundamental idea in the following characteristic sentence (I quote from the English translation of his *La Science Economique*) : " Commercial and Financial Crises are produced, not by over-production, but by over-consumption."[1]

Perhaps it may be claimed that a doctrine which gained such wide acceptance right at the beginning of the systematic study of industrial fluctuations cannot be as much opposed to sound common sense as it seems to appear to many to-day after a century of propaganda in favour of under-consumptionist explanations. That these early attempts did not have a more lasting success was probably due to the vague meaning of the various capital concepts which they had taken from the City jargon of the time. It is not difficult to see that with this very imperfect conceptual apparatus the adherents of this theory must have found it difficult to explain convincingly what they had rightly seen and to defend their accounts against criticisms. Even to-day we have not yet quite outgrown the stage in which the ambiguity—or rather lack—of meaning of the various concepts of capital which we still employ is a constant obstacle to real understanding. This is not least true of the term of " scarcity of capital " itself, and of the closely related concept of " free capital " to which it refers. Even if we connect fairly clear ideas with the term " scarcity of free capital," and even if the term is often used with advantage, nevertheless

---

[1] Yves Guyot, *Principles of Social Economy*, London, 1884, p. 249. For a slightly fuller account of these theories of the middle of the nineteenth century see the appendix to the third chapter of the second edition of *Prices and Production*, 1934.

it is in a sense misleading and will easily lead one to ask meaningless questions. The difficulty is that the term appears to refer to some single, measurable entity, some amount of money or " subsistence fund " which represents the " free capital " and which in real life simply does not exist. What we actually mean when we speak of scarcity or abundance of free capital is simply that the distribution of demand between consumers' goods and capital goods compared with the supply of these two kinds of goods is either relatively favourable or relatively unfavourable to the former.

VI

More important, however, is another difficulty connected with the traditional concepts of capital. It is this difficulty which seems to me to necessitate a restatement of the Wicksell-Mises theory of industrial fluctuations in the form which I have tried to sketch in this lecture. Prevailing ideas about how capital would normally be kept quantitatively intact in changing circumstances suggested the notion that a period of intense investment activity followed by a period when the value of much of the capital so created was destroyed might be treated as periods of alternating accumulation and decumulation of capital. For most practical purposes this may indeed represent a fairly adequate description of the real facts. Theoretically this way of approach appeared particularly attractive because it seemed to make it possible to describe the conditions of a stable equilibrium in the way which at the present moment is very fashionable ; in terms of the correspondence between (net) saving and (net) investment. Yet the first serious attempts exactly to define these two magnitudes, which are supposed to correspond in some quantitative sense, proved that these concepts had by no means a very clear meaning. Both concepts depend, as can be easily shown, on a vague idea that capital is " normally " kept or preserved constant in some quantitative sense : savings being that part of income which is not consumed we have to know first what income is, that is, we have to determine what part of total (gross) receipts has to be deducted for the amortisation of capital ; and similarly we can determine the magnitude of new investments only if we first decide what amount of investment activity is required in order merely to maintain old capital. Whether we are able to decide what savings and what investment are depends therefore on whether we can give the idea of maintaining capital intact a clear and realistic meaning.

That this can be easily done is usually taken for granted ; in fact it seems to be regarded as so obvious, that a more careful study of the question has mostly been regarded as unnecessary and has hardly ever been attempted. As soon, however, as one makes any serious attempt to answer this question, one finds not only that the concept of the maintenance of capital has no definite meaning, but also that there is no reason to assume that even the most rational and intelligent entrepreneur will ever in dynamic conditions be either willing or able to keep his capital constant in any quantitative sense, that is with respect to any of the measurable properties of capital itself. How entrepreneurs will behave in particular circumstances and whether the value of the capital under their control will experience unexpected increases or decreases in value will, of course, depend on the wisdom and foresight of the entrepreneurs. But, as I hope to show more fully on another occasion,[1] even if we could assume that entrepreneurs possessed full knowledge of all the relevant future events there would be no reason to expect that they would act in such a manner as to keep the value of their capital (or any other measurable dimension of this capital itself—as distinguished from the income derived from it) at any particular figure.

If the " Wicksellian " theory of crises were really as dependent on the traditional concepts of saving and investment as would seem to appear from the extensive use of these terms in the current expositions of it, the considerations just advanced would constitute a grave objection to it. Fortunately, however, there is no such necessary connection between that theory and these concepts. In the form in which it has, tentatively and very sketchily, been restated in the earlier part of this lecture, it appears to me to be quite independent of any idea of absolute changes in the quantity of capital and therefore of the concepts of saving and investment in their traditional sense. The starting point for a fully developed theory of this kind would be (a) the intentions of all the consumers with respect to the way in which they wish to distribute at all the relevant dates all their resources (not merely their " income ") between current consumption and provision for future consumption, and (b) the separate and independent decisions of the

---

[1] Cf. now the article on the Maintenance of Capital, reprinted above.

entrepreneurs with respect to the amounts of consumers' goods which they plan to provide at these various dates. Correspondence between these two groups of decisions would be characteristic of the kind of equilibrium which we now usually describe as a state where savings are equal to investments and with which the idea of an equilibrium rate of interest is connected. A rate of interest below that equilibrium rate would then induce entrepreneurs to devote a smaller share of the available resources to production for current consumption than the share of the income earned by these resources actually spent on consumption. This may mean that entrepreneurs lengthen the investment period by more than is justified by the voluntary "saving" of the entrepreneurs in the usual (net) sense of the term, or that they do not shorten the existing processes of production sufficiently to take full account of the "impatience" of the consumers (that is, in the usual terminology, of their desire to consume capital). It need not therefore be capital consumption in the absolute sense of the term, which is the essential characteristic of a crisis (as I have myself suggested on earlier occasions) but merely that the consumers demand a more rapid supply of consumers' goods than is possible in view of the decisions of the entrepreneurs as to the form and volume of their investments. Practically this correction probably makes little difference, but theoretically the statement of the theory can be made unobjectionable only if we free it from any reference to the absolute quantity of capital.

VII

It is scarcely possible to give in a short lecture more than a mere sketch of the developments taking place at the moment in trade cycle theory. And I need hardly add that in my view this development is still very far from complete and that what we can say to-day must necessarily be tentative and will probably undergo much further revision as time goes on. But even when at last we are able to state this particular argument in a more unobjectionable and convincing form than we can to-day, this will not mean an end but only a beginning. Even when we have answered the question how entrepreneurs will react to the expectations of particular price changes there will remain the much more difficult and important question of what determines the expectations of entrepreneurs and particularly of how such expectations will be affected by any given change of present prices. All these questions are still a more or less unworked field in which the first pioneer work has been done by one or two Scandinavian economists. And while I cannot quite agree with Professor Myrdal when he alleges that in my theory there is no room for the role played by expectations[1]—to show how important a place they do play was in fact one of the purposes of this lecture— I am on the other hand in complete agreement with him when he stresses the great importance of this element in the further development of the theory of industrial fluctuations. I have no doubt that in this

[1] Cf. G. Myrdal, Der Gleichgewichtsbegriff als Instrument der geldtheoretischen Analyse, *Beiträge zur Geldtheorie*, Ed. by F. A. Hayek, Vienna, 1933, p. 385.

field the whole complex of the theory of uncertainty and risk, to which Scandinavian economists have recently given so much attention, will become increasingly important.[1]

---

[1] See in this connection J. R. Hicks, "Gleichgewicht und Konjunktur," *Zeitschrift für Nationalökonomie*, Vol. IV, No. 4, 1933, and A Suggestion for Simplifying the Theory of Money, *Economica*, February, 1935.

V

SAVING[1]

THE original meaning of the term saving, keeping or preserving something for future use, has gradually been extended to cover a number of different activities more or less directly connected with the original sense of the word. As is so frequently the case with discussions of economic concepts our first task must therefore be, not just to assign one definite meaning to the term, but to isolate the different concepts attached to it and to preserve them, under this or other names, as instruments of analysis. The first complication arises from the fact that once it has been decided upon to postpone an act of consumption it will often be more profitable not to just keep the goods thus saved but to use the interval till they will be needed in order to produce such goods by more efficient but more time-consuming methods. This will involve a temporary transformation of the resources saved into new forms, an accumulation of productive capital, and once this stage is reached, there arises the first difficulty about the meaning of saving, that is whether here any particular decision to postpone a possible act of

[1] This is a reprint of the original manuscript of the article on Saving prepared for the *Encyclopædia of the Social Sciences* in 1933. It appeared with considerable editorial emendations and abridgments in Vol. XIII of that work in 1934.

consumption constitutes really new saving or whether it merely means that the results of old saving (the capital already accumulated) is maintained. At the same time this possibility of using the results cf saving in order to increase the product of current efforts will induce people to repeat the process of investing continuously and ultimately to treat the amount saved not as a reserve for future consumption but as a permanent source of revenue.

Even at this early stage in the development saving and investment become distinct activities ; even an isolated individual may save without investing ; but the distinction assumes much greater importance when we consider the process of saving in a money economy. It will still be possible here that someone may keep *in natura* a stock of commodities which he expects to need in the future. But the income which he may either currently consume or save will, in the first instance, consist of money and the immediate choice he will have to make will be between holding this money and investing it in order to get a return. In this situation, savings which are not invested assume a special significance which has prominently figured in all discussion on saving. The possibility that savings may be neither invested nor kept *in natura* but may take the form of money hoards creates further difficulties because it will be the cause of differences between saving (and also capital) in the individual sense and in the social sense. It would probably be better to avoid using the term with respect to society as a whole. Since, however, this practice has become so firmly established, it is important to realise that saving in the social sense is really a separate phenomenon—the increase of wealth or the formation of capital—of which individual saving is but one possible cause.

But, although saving is not synonymous with the formation of capital but merely the most important cause which normally leads to this result, it is impossible usefully to discuss saving without at the same time considering much that properly belongs only to the wider concept. To begin with, saving cannot be defined without some reference to the normal process of reproduction of capital ; it would be difficult to draw the line between that source of the supply of capital which can be described as saving proper and that which cannot ; nor is there any established usage as regards terminology. And many of the problems which have generally been discussed under the heading of saving refer either to the relation between saving and investing or else to the process of capital formation in general irrespective of whether it is due to saving proper or not.

Once we have recognised the necessity of distinguishing in all cases (except in that of saving *in natura*) between the activities which provide the means of investment (one of which is saving proper) and the activity of investment, we still have to make further distinctions between the various activities of the first kind—all of which are often loosely termed saving. The most convenient classification of the sources of the supply of new capital is probably that proposed by Professor Röpke, which can be roughly translated as follows :

I.   Saving *in natura*.
II.   Saving by means of money :
      1—individual (voluntary) saving,

2—corporate (voluntary) saving,

3—collective (compulsory) saving,

4—monetary (compulsory) saving.[1]

Of these different types of " saving," only II, 1, is generally understood by the more familiar use of the term saving. II, 2, referring to the reinvestment of undistributed profits of corporations has recently become more familiar and is now commonly included under " savings," although the voluntary character of the decision to save on the part of those who might otherwise have consumed the profits remains somewhat doubtful. Where the means for investment are raised by taxation (II, 3) the contrast between this sort of " saving " and what is ordinarily understood by this term is even stronger ; while in the case of II, 4 (now familiar under the name of *forced saving*), the peculiar characteristic is that the money for investment is not provided by any kind of saving but is created for the purpose. A sort of " saving " only occurs here when, in consequence of a diversion of resources from the production of consumers' goods to the production of capital goods, the current supply of consumers' goods is reduced. But the use of the term saving in this connection must be regarded as an instance of the misleading practice of treating the term as equivalent to " capital formation."

Further difficulties arise in connection with the distinction between net and gross saving. Once any capital is in existence its owners will constantly have to decide whether to reinvest enough of its proceeds

---

[1] W. Röpke, *Zur Theorie der Kapitalbildung*, Tübingen, 1929. In the German original Professor Röpke's classification is perhaps more satisfactory since in all cases except II, 1, he uses the equivalent of " formation of capital " instead of " saving."

to maintain the stock of capital intact which involves a new decision of whether to postpone consumption or not to do so. It has become customary to consider as savings proper only savings out of net income, after allowance has been made for the maintenance of capital, a usage which has sometimes led to the dangerous confusion of the supply of new free capital with the total free capital available for investment. It is extremely difficult to draw a clear line of demarcation between the two, for this would require a satisfactory definition of what is meant by maintaining capital intact, particularly under conditions of technical progress, a task which has not yet been accomplished. The difficulties here arise already with the savings of an individual but to an even greater extent in connection with savings in the social sense. In the latter case the gross total of individual savings has to be reduced by the amount of old savings which have been deliberately used up for consumption and there is in addition the difficult question of whether to treat involuntary capital losses as a further negative item which has to be deducted before we arrive at the figure for the net saving, which constitutes the supply of free capital available for new investment.

Any historical treatment of saving is faced not only with the difficulties arising out of the difference between saving and the creation of capital or the increase of wealth in the aggregate, but in addition with the problem of distinguishing between the causes of this and the causes of the concentration of wealth in the hands of particular persons. Much confusion has been caused in historical investigations by the lack of clear distinctions in this respect. As regards the supply of savings available for the creation of new capital equipment the first point to be stressed is that the regular investment of savings is a comparatively new phenomenon. While the storing of consumers' goods *in natura* has probably never been of very great importance (the occasional public storage of grain, etc., against famine excepted), the hoarding of precious metals must be regarded as the normal form of saving throughout most of history and is still customary among most people of non-European stock. It would certainly be untrue historically to say that the growth of this form of saving is a consequence of the introduction of money ; it would probably be more true to say that the particular suitability of the precious metals as a " store of value " made them generally acceptable as a medium of exchange. Until the Industrial Revolution hoarding of money remained the normal form of saving in all cases where the saver himself was not in a position to use capital productively. In other words, throughout antiquity, the Middle Ages, and for some time thereafter, even when savings were invested this did not mean as a rule the separation of the saver and the investor ; and where individual savings were not employed by their owner as productive capital, either because they were too small or for other reasons, he normally had no other alternative but to hoard them. Even entrepreneurs seeking to provide for a time when they should have ceased directly to employ capital in production or trade often accumulated hoards ; and as late as the beginning of the eighteenth century we hear of London merchants on their retirement taking a chest of gold coin with them to the

country with the intention of gradually drawing on
that hoard for the rest of their lives.

Until the industrial revolution new capital came
mainly from the reinvestment of profits by entrepreneurs. Long distance trade was the most important
source of the accumulation of capital in the sense
of new productive equipment. The other sources generally mentioned in this connection, particularly landed
property, had probably more to do with the concentration of wealth than with the creation of capital. The
most important early instrumentalities of profitable
investment for the non-entrepreneurs, which offered a
permanent source of income to new classes of savers
and thus encouraged the development of the saving
habit—government loans, annuities and mortgages—
represented investments only from the point of view
of the individual ; their proceeds were normally used
for consumption purposes and did not result in the
formation of new capital. It is probable that even in
the earlier stages of modern manufacture—in England
of the second half of the eighteenth and the first quarter
of the nineteenth century—relatively little of the capital
required came from outside savings, although the
growth of banking institutions had provided an agency
for their collection. It was only with the development
of the modern capital market during the railway booms
of the 1820's and 1830's and with the simultaneous and
subsequent growth of banking and other investing
institutions that the modern relation between the
individual small saver and the entrepreneur-investor
was established. In the second quarter of the century
the desire to collect and fructify not only current
savings but also old accumulated hoards of money

became one of the leading ideas of economic policy and the main cause of repeated waves of credit expansion. In the period preceding the World War hoarding of coin, except as a temporary phenomenon during depression, had disappeared from modern industrial societies.

But while the depositing of such savings with a bank or savings bank must still be regarded as the normal way in which savings are made available for investment, even before the Great War and still more so since, the importance of specialised institutions has steadily grown which are more adapted to the particular needs of the individual saver. Besides life insurance, as the most important, building societies and similar institutions facilitating saving for a particular purpose ought to be mentioned.

What has just been said about the disappearance of hoarding is true at least of the hoarding of hand to hand money. It was generally assumed that since people tend to bring any sum saved to a bank or similar institution, all savings would soon be invested. But in so far as people already hold their normal balances for current expenditure in the form of bank deposits, saving may simply mean that they will leave these deposits unused or at best that they will transfer them from a checking (current) to a savings (deposit) account. As both A. C. Pigou and D. H. Robertson have pointed out, saving in this case will not necessarily result in additional investments by the banks ; only if the form of deposits is changed and if, as in the United States, reserves held against time (savings) deposits are smaller than those against demand deposits, will at least a part of the new savings be used for new investments. Unless the banks create additional credits for investment purposes to the same extent that the holders of deposits have ceased to use them for current expenditure, the effect of such saving is essentially the same as that of hoarding and has all the undesirable deflationary consequences attaching to the latter.

The effects usually imputed to saving are, however, imputed not to savings which are hoarded but to those which are invested. Such investment means, if the capital created by it is to remain intact, that a quantity of intermediate products, corresponding to the amount of factors invested, will be permanently withheld from consumption and that with the help of this additional capital the output of consumers' goods will be augmented but their cost per unit decreased. In a situation where all factors are already employed when the new investment is being made, this will mean that the average investment period is being lengthened, fewer consumers' goods must be produced during the transition period and less can therefore be consumed. Because of the decreased expenditure on consumers' goods, the prices of consumers' goods will tend to fall ; thereby the necessary curtailment of the output of consumers' goods is brought about and the factors of production required for an increased output of capital goods are set free. Even where saving leads not to an increase in the average period of investment (*i.e.*, an increase of the amount of capital per head) but only to the provision of equipment for factors previously not employed, those factors which were already employed and which provided the savings out of their income must reduce their consumption in order to remunerate the new factors until the product of the latter is ready. While in this case only consumption per head—and not total consumption—must be reduced, in a case where saving leads only to the investment for longer periods of factors already employed, the absolute rate of consumption will have to be reduced temporarily in order to spread the existing output over a longer period, after which the product of the factors now being invested will become available.

The second effect of new investment, the reduction of cost per unit, is important because it shows that the increase in output at a later stage is due not to the fact that the product of a greater quantity of factors then comes on the market but to the fact that, with the help of the additional capital, the original factors produce more than before. The income of all these factors is therefore still equal to the cost of production of the current output and sufficient to take it off the market at remunerative prices. Serious disturbances, however, may follow large and unforeseen fluctuations in the rate of saving and, in consequence of the relative increase in the demand for consumers' goods, an increase of investment in excess of saving proper by means of additional credits.

Because of a misunderstanding of the process through which the temporary reduction of consumption brings about a permanent increase in current output (or a reduction of cost per unit), saving has since early times been persistently blamed for causing trade depressions. " Under-consumption " or " over-saving " explanations of trade slumps were at the basis of many of the earlier discussions of unproductive expenditure and of luxury consumption. Since Malthus and Lauderdale these theories have always had some following, particularly among socialist thinkers, and have gained wide popularity during depressions. In recent years they have been reflected mainly in the notion of " maintaining purchasing power " of consumers and in this form have been strongly supported by groups advocating stabilisation of the price level of consumers' goods. It is becoming increasingly clear, however, that these theories are false and that there are only the three special cases—hoarding, violent fluctuations in the rate of saving and forced saving through credit expansion—in which excessive saving may be said to cause depression. Apart from these cases it is doubtful whether there is any sense in which the rate of saving may be absolutely too high or too low. A " general glut " in consequence of too ample a supply of means for investment cannot occur so long as there are still unused opportunities for investment which offer a positive rate of interest. And even if the demand for capital in the form of new productive equipment were not very elastic, the demand for durable consumer goods is practically inexhaustible. What is commonly meant by over-investment is not an excess of investment relative to the demand for the ultimate product, but an excessive launching of new undertakings which need for their completion or utilisation more capital than is available ; in other words, " over-investment " implies not too much saving but too little. Nor can it be said that over-saving may reduce the value of the product of the investment below the point where it justifies the sacrifice involved in the act of saving. This thesis, frequently advanced, offers a curious contrast to the equally current proposition that "under-estimation of future wants" prevents an increase of saving to the point where the rate of interest would fall to zero. Both views imply the existence of a normal scale of preference between present and future goods, by which the actual preferences of the individuals can be gauged. There is, however, no other basis for the determination of the relative utilities to an.individual at different moments of time but his actual preference, shown at the moment when he decides either to consume or to postpone consumption.

To say that a person underestimates his future wants, even if he saves considerable amounts in order to increase his future income (as is suggested by many forms of the time-preference theories of interest) is just as unjustifiable as to say that he saves too much. Both statements are based on the observer's opinion of what he considers the appropriate distribution of resources over time.

While there is no "just balance between saving and consumption" in the usual sense and while saving at any stable rate can be absorbed without real difficulty, it is very likely that in a dynamic economy—a society with a growing population, advancing technology and a modern banking system—saving at a continuously high rate is an important safeguard of stability. This will not only facilitate the absorption of additional population, and minimise the friction connected with technical progress and shifts of demand, but will probably also tend to mitigate disturbances arising from fluctuations in credit. In the absence of a sufficient supply of new capital any unusually profitable opening for investment will tend to attract capital from other uses and so to enforce extensive readjustments ; the introduction of labour-saving inventions may lead also to a lowering of wages. With a rapid increase in the capital supply, such readjustments can be effected much more smoothly or obviated altogether. Similarly, the greater the investment based on voluntary saving, the smaller will be the relative variation in the total rate of investment caused by a given rate of credit expansion. Even the inherent instability of capital created by forced saving might be counteracted if sufficient voluntary savings became available to provide a real basis for this capital.

What the actual volume of saving is depends upon willingness and capacity to save. The factors which affect an individual's willingness to save are the regularity and certainty of his income, the security of the investment opportunities available to him, and the possibility of investing in his own business. It is worth mentioning here that the systems of social insurance which, while securing incomes in old age and providing for sickness, accidents and unemployment, provide for payments out of accumulated revenues rather than accumulated reserves, are, no doubt, a very important factor decreasing the aggregate supply of savings.

It seems that in the short run the willingness to save varies very little and that it is particularly not much affected in the aggregate by changes in the rate of interest. This is mainly due to the fact that while to some people a rise in the rate of interest provides an increased incentive to save, other people who want to accumulate a definite amount for a given purpose (life insurance, house purchase, etc.) need to save less if the rate of interest is higher. While for these reasons it is very difficult to form a clear opinion as to the elasticity of the aggregate supply of savings, it is probably safe to say that, in so far as changes in the willingness to save are concerned, this elasticity is very low. This does not mean, however, that changes in the rate of interest may not affect the aggregate supply of savings very considerably in a different way, namely *via* the capacity to save of the various individuals. There can be little doubt that in general people with a given attitude towards saving will save a higher percentage of a larger than of a smaller income. A transfer of income from classes with a smaller to classes with a greater income (as might be brought about by a change in the rate of interest) is therefore likely to increase the supply of savings. And a rise in aggregate incomes which might be brought about by the same cause, will, of course, have the same effect.

VI

THE PRESENT STATE AND IMMEDIATE PROSPECTS OF THE STUDY OF INDUSTRIAL FLUCTUATIONS[1]

HOWEVER one defines *Konjunkturforschung* there can be little question that its present state, as well as its prospects and tasks in the immediate future, is determined more by the extent of our present understanding of the causes operating in this field than by the amount of descriptive material at our disposal—the latter representing the constantly changing object to which we have to apply our theoretical knowledge. In the following attempt to discuss the " present state and the immediate prospects of *Konjunkturforschung*" this term will therefore be interpreted in the sense of the general theory of industrial fluctuations and not as referring to the technique and method of current observation practised by the various economic services.

It can hardly be denied that this branch of economic theory has made considerable progress during the last ten years and that the state of our knowledge is considerably more satisfactory than a generation or even a few years ago ; and it is probably also true that there is comparatively more agreement among

[1] Translated from *Der Stand und die nächste Zukunft der Konjunktur forschung, Festschrift für Arthur Spiethoff*, Munich, 1933.

theoretical economists interested in this field than among the contemporaries who are largely interested in factual description. At least in so far as the factors determining the boom and the immediate causes of the crisis are concerned there is to-day no fundamental difference between the views of say Spiethoff, Cassel, Wicksell, and Mises and a large group of writers who in other respects hold very different views—J. Åkerman, B. M. Anderson, Breasciani-Turroni, Budge, Eucken, Fanno, Fasiani, Haberler, Halm, Landauer, Machlup, Morgenstern, Robertson, Robbins, Röpke, Strigl, and Adolf Weber. The achievement of the last few years which must not be underestimated is the clearer insight we have at last gained into a process often vaguely seen but never before adequately described or explained : the process by which misdirections of capital caused by credit expansion will in the end, when consumers' demand grows too rapidly, lead to a scarcity of capital which makes it impossible to use a large part of the equipment which has been adapted to a state where capital was more abundant. The most important advance in this field is undoubtedly the more careful analysis of this state of " simultaneous scarcity and abundance " (Spiethoff), which is somewhat inadequately described by the terms "scarcity of capital " or " scarcity of circulating capital," an analysis which has led to the conclusion that this scarcity of capital is simply relative over-consumption. In addition to the demonstration, which this implies, that the underconsumption theories are logically indefensible, the most important step in this direction was the regained understanding of the function of the rate of interest— and particularly of its necessity even in a stationary state—which had been badly obscured by the temporary fashion of interest theories based on purely "dynamic" considerations or merely on considerations of banking liquidity.[1] Perhaps not much less important for the increasing agreement on fundamentals was the abandonment of the idea, based on the more naïve monetary theories of the trade cycle, that all that was required to abolish industrial fluctuations was the stabilisation of the price level ; this last advance, however, was probably due less to the theoretical argument of a few economists than to the bad disappointment caused by the crisis of 1929 following a period of fairly stable prices.

This important agreement on fundamentals must, however, neither deceive us into disregarding the important differences between the formulations by the various authors, which indeed are such that in many instances it is difficult to recognise the fundamental similarity of their views, nor make us forget that even the common general outline of these explanations still contains problems the solution of which has hardly yet been attempted. We have as yet very little of that developed theory of the formation, maintenance, transformation and consumption of capital which takes account of the different degrees of mobility and adaptability of the different kinds of capital goods and their distribution between the various stages of production

---

[1] This was, of course, written before Mr. Keynes with his *General Theory* started in this country a fashion very similar to that which had prevailed in Germany in the nineteen-twenties. The statement in the text refers to Schumpeter's "dynamic" theory of interest and particularly to L. A. Hahn's *Volkswirtschaftliche Theorie des Bankkredits* (1920), which contains a discussion of "the rate of interest as a price for the loss of liquidity" which at the time attracted much attention and gave rise to extensive discussions.

which we need if we are to be able to translate the abstract scheme of our explanation into more concrete terms. To give only one example of how little we really know about the dynamics of capitalistic production, it may be mentioned that even such a fundamental concept as that of " maintaining capital intact " is still exceedingly vague and obscure in its meaning—although, of course, problems like that of the correspondence between (new) savings and (new) investments, which play such a great role in all the theories belonging to this group, can hardly be intelligently discussed without a clear conception of what is meant by maintaining capital intact.

But even if we can hope that these conceptual difficulties still inherent in the present formulation of our theory will be gradually cleared up in the course of further discussion, there are undeniably other chapters of the explanations of industrial fluctuations which are in a much less satisfactory state. As soon as we proceed from the causes of the crisis proper to the explanation of the more advanced stages of the depression and of the process of liquidation which restores some sort of equilibrium, that is as soon as we turn to the problems which at the present moment are most intensively discussed, we find hardly any agreement between the various writers and I doubt whether anyone can pride himself on having a clear picture of these complicated processes. Yet it seems to me as if the better insight we have gained into the crucial problems of the crisis proper had also improved prospects of progress in this field. If this process of liquidation and adjustment which follows the crisis is still largely unexplored, this is probably due to the fact that it can be understood only on the basis of a correct explanation of the crisis ; and if there is reason to be optimistic about recent progress on the latter point, we are probably also justified in now expecting more rapid progress in the former field. But the attempts (of which Mr. Keynes' *Treatise on Money* is probably the most interesting[1]) made so far to clear up these (in a methodological sense) secondary complications which arise during the depression, all suffer from the defect that they proceed from an assumed position of disequilibrium without a sufficient explanation how this has arisen.

How confused ideas still are with respect to the problems of the liquidation and readjustment of the economic system after a crisis is well illustrated by the vague and indefinite way in which in recent years financial journalists and others have discussed the problem of liquidation of the present depression. The analysis of the crisis shows that, once an excessive increase of the capital structure has proved insupportable and has led to a crisis, profitability of production can be restored only by considerable changes in relative prices, reductions of certain stocks, and transfers of means of production to other uses. In connection with these changes, liquidations of firms in a purely financial sense of the word may be inevitable, and their postponement may possibly delay the process of liquidation in the first, more general sense ; but this is a separate

[1] For a discussion of Mr. Keynes' views and the way in which confusions inherent in his fundamental concepts have vitiated his comprehensive attempt to clear up those complications cf. my " Reflections on the Pure Theory of Money of Mr. J. M. Keynes," *Economica*, August and November, 1931, and February, 1932.

and special phenomenon which in recent discussions has been stressed rather excessively at the expense of the more fundamental changes in prices, stocks, etc. A theoretical problem of great importance which needs to be elucidated in this connection is the significance, for this process of liquidation, of the rigidity of prices and wages, which since the great war has undoubtedly become very considerable. There can be little question that these rigidities tend to delay the process of adaptation and that this will cause a " secondary " deflation which at first will intensify the depression but ultimately will help to overcome these rigidities. The main problems in this connection, on which opinions are still diametrically opposed, are, firstly, whether this process of deflation is merely an evil which has to be combated, or whether it does not serve a necessary function in breaking these rigidities, and, secondly, whether the persistence of these deflationary tendencies proves that the fundamental maladjustment of prices still exists, or whether, once that process of deflation has gathered momentum, it may not continue long after it has served its initial function.

Such an induced[1] process of deflation (*i.e.*, a process not deliberately brought about by the central banks and which might occur equally under a purely metallic currency) raises problems of the most interesting kind. Quite apart from the fact which has always been emphasised, probably rightly, by men of practical experience, that it is very questionable whether such

---

[1] Since this was written I have learnt that the term " induced " deflation has been used by American economists, probably more logically, in the exactly opposite sense, to describe a deflation induced by the banking system. " Spontaneous " deflation would probably have been a better term for what is meant in the text.

a deflation can be successfully combated by the ordinary means of central banking policy, it is quite possible that a general expectation of a continued fall of prices may have very peculiar effects and may invert certain rules which apply under normal conditions : it is for instance at least conceivable that a fall of the prices of consumers' goods, which creates the expectation of still lower prices in the future, may make the current production of consumers' goods appear more profitable than investments which will help the production of consumers' goods in the future, and thus will lead to a reduction of the proportion of capital used in the production of consumers' goods. This influence of price expectations on the structure of production and the closely connected questions of changes in the velocity of circulation of money or the cash balances held are problems which urgently require study within the general framework of a theory of intertemporal price relationships. What is needed is a fusion of the results of the study of three groups of problems, up till now discussed in separate sections of economic theory : the capital problem which results from the fact that cash balances are capital from the point of view of the individual but not for society as a whole ; the monetary problem of changes in the velocity of circulation ; and in price theory the problem of intertemporal exchange relationships. It is only from such a development that we can expect that advance in the theory of interest, making it more realistic and concrete, which I have discussed in another place.[1]

[1] *Monetary Theory and the Trade Cycle*, Ch. V. Perhaps I might also mention here that it was essentially the considerations indicated in the text which have led me to collect a number of important

Finally, as the last and most important of the problems which urgently require solution, we might mention the mechanism of the re-absorption of the unemployed productive forces—men as well as equipment—at the end of a depression and particularly the role of credit expansion in this process. Although the general principles raise here no great difficulties, and although in particular it is probably generally recognised to-day that the need for additional credit in this connection is a genuine need for additional capital, it must be admitted that the traditional analysis of the effects of credit expansion cannot be applied to this case without considerable modifications. The reason for this is that in this situation the expansion of credit for investment purposes will not lead to a diversion of productive resources into more "roundabout" processes of production with a consequent decrease of the current output of consumers' goods, but merely to a redistribution of the available supply of consumers' goods among a greater amount of factors of production. The re-employment of equipment and men, to employ whom it has not been profitable before, is made possible in this case by a reduction of real wages.[1] This reduction of real wages through a rise in the prices of consumers' goods compared with such a

contributions to these problems, which had not been available in one of the generally understood languages, in a volume called *Beiträge zur Geldtheorie* (by M. Fanno, M. W. Holtrop, J. G. Koopmans, G. Myrdal and K. Wicksell, Vienna, 1933).

[1] As will be apparent from the first essay in this collection I believe now that this statement is incorrect as far as the beginning of the recovery is concerned ; it applies only to the more advanced stages of the boom, when the supply of consumers' goods begins to fall short of demand. In the following sentence of the text "profits" should be substituted for "interest."

reduction brought about by a lowering of money wages
has, however, the disadvantage that this rise of prices of
consumers' goods, caused by the increase of demand
before supply has increased, will lead to a rise in the
rate of interest. As, however, in this situation money
wages are not likely to rise in consequence of a rise in
the prices of consumers' goods, the effects of credit
expansion will be less harmful than under conditions
of full employment. It is at least conceivable that in
this case, in analogy to the case of an expected continued
fall of the prices of consumers' goods considered before,
the rise of prices accompanying the increasing employment will create the expectation of still higher prices in
the future and thus stimulate investment.

All this is, of course, no real attempt at a solution of
these problems, but merely an indication of the lines
on which such a solution must be sought. And among
the problems which now urgently require a solution,
the effects of a credit expansion under dynamic
conditions certainly takes first place, just because we
are now fairly clear as to what these effects are in an
otherwise stationary system. It is not to be expected
that further research in this direction will force us to
change our views on the general principles involved.
But as a further example of the unexpected conclusions to which we may be led if we apply these
general principles to more complicated conditions,
some further remarks may be added here on the
effects of credit expansion in a progressive society.
This case is particularly interesting because in a society
where population and capital are growing credit
expansion could only be avoided at the price of a
continuous fall not only of the prices of consumers'

goods but also of the factors of production, *i.e.*, incomes, which would undoubtedly create very serious frictions. In an economic system with a high rate of voluntary saving it is, however, by no means impossible that at the critical moment, when credit expansion has to be slowed down and the further increase of incomes and the demand for consumers' goods relatively to investment threatens to lead to a crisis, the continued saving at a high rate may more than offset the tendency towards an increase of consumption and thus prevent the crisis. The conditions under which this might be the case would be not only that credit expansion has not proceeded at too fast a rate, and that it is slowed down very gradually, but also that the part of the supply of free capital which is due to voluntary savings is large compared with the part due to an expansion of credit. If these conditions are satisfied the result might be that for a time the current voluntary savings will be used to take over, as it were, the capital created by means of forced saving ; and current savings would then have to serve, not to make further new investment possible, but merely to maintain capital which has been formed in anticipation of these savings. And although even in this case the forced saving will not have increased the total amount of capital that can be accumulated in the long run, it will at least not lead to the crisis which would be the inevitable consequence if it were not for the continued voluntary saving. It is possible that this fact explains why at the present moment (1932) certain countries with a high rate of saving (in particular, France) are in a less depressed condition than most others.

The list of such problems yet waiting for a solution

could, of course, be continued almost indefinitely. But this fact does not detract from the value of the progress of our knowledge in recent years, of which we have spoken at the beginning of this article, nor does it give support to the views of those who object to the simplified constructions and abstract deductions from which we start and usually impute to those who use them an unwarranted neglect of the further complications. If we are now in a position to attack these further problems with a chance of success, this is mainly due to the fact that we are at last in a position to state the skeleton of our explanation in a logically consistent manner. Nobody can hope that we shall soon be in a position to give a final answer to all the important questions in this field. The concrete forms in which these phenomena manifest themselves in the real world are far too complex and variable, and the process by which theoretical and descriptive work mutually supply each other with questions and their answers is far too slow to justify much optimism in this respect. Our success in recasting an important part of traditional theory into a logically consistent system and in refuting at the same time some of the most widely held fallacies is no small achievement and should prove a great help in further developments. This confidence need not be shaken by certain deplorable tendencies in the economic literature of the most recent times. It cannot be denied that the present crisis, as is true of almost all earlier crises, has enormously swollen the literature of our subject, and that not only errors of the most primitive kind have been revived by outsiders, but that even competent scholars appear to have lost their heads and in their anxiety to help quickly have proposed remedies which are hardly compatible with their theoretical views. But once the problems of the present crisis have ceased to be as pressing as they are now, further research will not only have new important material at its disposal, but will also be able to base itself on a stream of secured knowledge which may be temporarily submerged but certainly not stopped by the present flood of dilettante literature.

VII

A NOTE ON THE DEVELOPMENT OF THE DOCTRINE OF " FORCED SAVING "[1]

THE enhanced interest in the problem of " Forced Saving," due to recent developments in the theory of industrial fluctuations, has led to the discovery of so many more or less distinct allusions to that subject in the works of earlier writers that the sketch of the development of that doctrine, which I attempted in the first chapter of my *Prices and Production*[2] has rapidly become out of date. Since, in addition to the several early references to this problem which have recently been noticed by other writers, I have now discovered what is, perhaps, their common source, it may be worth while to redraw my previous sketch of the development of this doctrine.

Although it is impossible at the present time to show conclusively whether or in what way Jeremy Bentham's teaching on this point was disseminated at the time when he formulated his opinions, it now appears to me to be practically certain that the earliest—and also the

---

[1] Reprinted from *The Quarterly Journal of Economics*, Vol. XLVII, November, 1932.
[2] *Prices and Production*, London, 1931, pp. 17–19. Part of the material used in the following note has already been mentioned in the German edition of the same work, published shortly after the English edition under the title of *Preise und Produktion*, Vienna,. 1931, pp. 18–20.

clearest and most elaborate—statement of this theory is to be found in the writings of that author. In a passage which received its final form in 1804—though it was probably sketched much earlier, and not published until 1843 in his *Manual of Political Economy*[1]—he deals in some detail with the phenomenon which he calls " Forced Frugality." He seems to have hit upon this idea in exactly the connection in which one would expect it to occur first ; and his influence on almost all economists of the early nineteenth century probably accounts for the fact that the idea is mentioned again and again in this period in very similar terms, even though his own statement did not appear in print until a much later date.

It might be expected that the author of the Defence of Usury, who was an acute observer of the effects of the Fixation of Prices[2] and who had adopted as his *leitmotiv* for the study of the art of Political Economy the statement that " industry is limited by capital," would turn his attention to the problem of whether government measures might not lead to an increase of that capital. Indeed, the first example of the " broad

---

[1] The *Works of Jeremy Bentham*, published under the superintendence of his executor, John Bowring, Vol. III, Edinburgh, 1843, pp. 31–84. The Manual, as there reprinted, though the only edition which is reasonably complete, obviously does not represent a complete manuscript which Bentham intended to be published in that form, but rather a compilation by the editor from different manuscripts and some fragments published by Dumont. Nor is it true, as is frequently asserted, that all parts of the Manual, as printed there, date back to 1793. A cursory inspection of the Bentham manuscripts in University College, London, shows that the material in the published Manual belongs to quite different periods and that there is, in addition to it, a good deal of apparently very interesting unpublished material. A critical edition of all the economic writings of Bentham is urgently needed.

[2] Cf. Manual, Ch. III, Sec. 22. *Works*, Ed. Bowring, iii, 66.

measures " of governments (*i.e.*, such measures as
" have for their object the augmentation of wealth
in all its shapes without distinction ") which Bentham
discusses among what he calls Non-agenda of the state,
is headed " Forced Frugality."[1]

" By raising money," he writes, " as other money is
raised, by taxes (the amount of which is taken by
individuals out of their expenditure on the score of
maintenance), government has it in its power to accelerate,
to an unexampled degree, the augmentation of the mass of
real wealth. By a proportionable sacrifice of present
comfort, it may make any addition that it pleases to the
mass of future wealth ; that is, to the increase of comfort
and security. But though it has it in its power to do this,
it follows not that it ought to exercise this power to
compel the community to make this sacrifice."

And after a lengthy discussion of this form of Forced
Frugality, which does not concern us here, Bentham
continues :—

" The effect of forced frugality is also produced by the
creating of paper money by government, or the suffering
of the creation of paper money by individuals. In this case,
the effect is produced by a species of indirect taxation,
which has hitherto passed almost unnoticed."

Bentham then proceeds to study, as example 2 of his
" broad measures " among the *non-agenda*, the effects
of increasing money in some detail. " Labour," he
begins, " and not money, is the real source of wealth."

" All hands being employed, and employed in the most
advantageous manner, wealth—real wealth—could admit
of no further increase ; but money would be increasable
ad infinitum. The effect of every increase of money
(understand, of the ratio of the quantity of money
employed in the purchase of things vendible, to the

[1] *Ibid.*, p. 44, Ch. III, Sec. 4.

quantity of things vendible for money) is to impose an unprofitable *income tax* on the incomes of all fixed incomists."[1]

" If, on the introduction of the additional money into circulation, it pass in the first instance into hands which employ it in the way of unproductive expenditure, the suffering from this tax remains altogether uncompensated ; if before it come into any hands of that description, it have come into hands by which it has been employed in the shape of capital, the suffering by the income tax is partly reduced and partly compensated. It is reduced by the mass of things vendible produced by means of it : a mass by the amount of which, were it not for the corresponding increase in the mass of money, the value of the mass of money would *pro tanto* have been increased, and the prices of things vendible decreased. It is in a certain degree, though in a very inadequate degree, compensated for by the same means ; viz., by the amount of the addition made to the quantity of sensible wealth—of wealth

[1] Here Bentham appends the following very interesting footnote, which is curious as an early attempt to estimate the quantitative importance of this phenomenon : " The following is an indication of the indirect income tax resulting from the increase of money : In Britain (anno 1801) money is about £72,000,000 ; income about £216,000,000 (72 : 216 : : 1 : 3). Each million added to *money* adds therefore *three* millions for ever to *pecuniary income ;* and this (setting aside the 15 per cent for ever—£150,000—for profit on the million if employed in the shape of capital) without addition to real income. If, in every year, £2,000,000 be added to money (*plus* £300,000 for an equivalent to the addition made as above to real wealth) then in 36 years (anno 1837) the nominal or pecuniary amount of a mass of real income equal to the amount of 1801, will be doubled, *i.e.*, become £432,000,000 ; to which will be added £10,800,000 for an equivalent to the intermediate addition to real wealth (£300,000 × 36). But the £432,000,000 of 1837, being worth not more than the £216,000,000 of 1801, each £100 of the £432,000,000 will be worth but £50 of the £216,000,000 ; that is, the income of each *fixed incomist* will, by that time, have been subjected to an indirect income tax of £50 per cent. He whose pecuniary income of 1837 is double what it is in 1801, will in point of *wealth* be neither a *gainer* nor a *loser* by the change. Not so in point of *comfort.* For by so much as he is a gainer in wealth the *one* way, by so much is he the loser in the *other ;* and by the nature and constitution of the human frame, sum for sum, enjoyment from *gain* is never equal to the suffering from loss."

possessing a value in the way of use. Here, as in the above case of forced frugality, national wealth is increased at the expense of national comfort and national justice."

After some further remarks on the same subject, which there is no need to quote here, Bentham continues :

"No sooner, however, does such additional sum of money pass on from the hands by which it is employed in the shape of capital, into those hands by which it is employed in adding to unproductive expenditure, than its operation in the way of making an addition to real wealth is at an end. No sooner does it go in addition to money employed in the purchase of articles for consumption, than its power of producing an addition to the mass of the matter of real wealth is at an end : thenceforward and for ever it keeps on contributing by its whole amount to the increase in prices, in the same manner as if from the mines it had come in the first instance into an unproductive hand, without passing through any productive one."

As an historical fact, however, Bentham thinks that

"It is a matter of uncertainty what part, and even whether any part (of the increase of wealth) has been produced by the addition to money, since without any such addition it might have been produced as well as by it."

Shortly after Bentham had given definite shape to his thoughts in 1804 (from his manuscripts it seems clear that he had been working on them at least as early as 1801—perhaps much earlier) he noticed that he had already been anticipated. On March 22nd, 1804, he wrote to his French editor, Dumont :

"I had been working at, and thought to have finished a concise view of the influence of money in the increase of wealth as a specimen of the 'Præcognita,' preparatory to the practical part—the Agenda and Non-agenda.

188 PROFITS, INTEREST AND INVESTMENT

But, just now, I got returned from Trail my Thornton and
your Wheatley ; and I see few ideas in my papers that
are not to be found somewhere or other in their books.
What I could hope to do would be little more than substituting method to chaos, and keeping clear of contra-
dictions, which are to be found in both, but more
particularly in Wheatley. The moral is that I should go
quietly back to Evidence. . . ."[1]

While Wheatley's *Remarks*[2] seem, however, to
contain nothing upon the problem which interests us
here, Thornton had indeed expressed similar thoughts
in the following paragraph of his *Paper Credit*[3] :

" It must also be admitted that, provided we assume
an excessive issue of paper to lift up, as it may for a time,
the costs of goods though not the price of labour, some
augmentation of stock will be the consequence ; for the
labourer according to this supposition, may be forced by

---

[1] See *Works*, Ed. Bowring, Vol. X, p. 413. Bentham had already
read Thornton two years before and had praised him highly in a
letter to Dumont dated June 28th, 1802. He wrote, " This is a book
of real merit—a controversy with him would be really instructive.
I have tumbled it over but very imperfectly, that not being the order
of the day, and for fear of calling off my attention, and absorbing
my capacity of exertion. But, one of these days, I may not improb-
ably grapple with him. Admitting all his facts with thanks—agreeing
with him in almost all his conclusions—but disputing with him what
seems (as far as I have yet seen) to be his most material conclusion,
viz., that paper money does more good than harm. Here is a book
of real instruction, if the French are wise enough to translate it ;
the style clear, plain, without ornament or pretension ; the reasoning
close." (*Ibid.*, p. 389.) Dumont seems to have taken the hint.
At least, the Bibliothèque Britannique of Geneva, where, in earlier
years, Dumont had published part of the Manual and other manuscripts of Bentham, published in its volumes XXI–XXIII (1802
et seq.) six long extracts from Thornton's book, announcing at the
same time a forthcoming French translation.
[2] John Wheatley, *Remarks on Currency and Commerce*, London,
1803.
[3] Henry Thornton, *An Enquiry into the Nature and Effects of the
Paper Credit of Great Britain*, London, 1802, p. 263. Attention has
already been drawn to this remark of Thornton by Prof. C. Bresciani-
Turroni, *Le Vicende del Marco Tedesco*, Milano, 1931, p. 240.

his necessity to consume fewer articles, though he may exercise the same industry. But this saving, as well as any additional one which may arise from a similar defalcation of the revenue of the unproductive members of the society will be attended with a proportional injustice and hardship."

The next and much more detailed exposition of this phenomenon which I have noticed—that of Malthus in his review of Ricardo's *High Price of Bullion*[1]—I have already quoted at some length in *Prices and Production*. Here I only want to draw the attention of the reader to the striking similarity between the phrasing of Malthus and that of Bentham. Since my mention of Malthus in this connection, my attention has been drawn to an almost simultaneous discussion of the same problem by Dugald Stewart which, however—like Bentham's contribution—did not appear in print until many years afterwards.[2] In a series of memoranda,

---

[1] *Edinburgh Review*, Vol. XVII, No. XXXIV, February, 1811, p.363 *et seq*. Cf. also Ricardo's reply in the appendix to the fourth edition of his pamphlet on *The High Price of Bullion*. " If such a distribution of the circulating medium were to take place, as to throw the command of the produce of the country chiefly into the hands of the productive classes—that is, if considerable portions of the currency were taken from the idle and those who live upon fixed incomes, and transferred to farmers, manufacturers and merchants, the proportion between capital and revenue would be greatly altered to the advantage of capital ; and, in a short time, the produce of the country would be greatly augmented.

" Whenever, in the actual state of things, a fresh issue of notes comes into the hands of those who mean to employ it in the prosecution and extension of profitable business, a difference in the distribution of the circulating medium takes place, similar in kind to that which has been last supposed ; and produces similar, though, of course, comparatively inconsiderable effects, in altering the proportion between capital and revenue in favour of the former." The continuation of the passage is quoted in *Prices and Production*, p. 18.

[2] Cf. *The Collected Works of Dugald Stewart*, Ed. by Sir William Hamilton, London, 1855, viii, 440–449. The reference to Dugald Stewart in this connection I owe to Prof. Jacob Viner.

which he wrote in 1811 for Lord Lauderdale,[1] on the *Bullion Report* and which were reprinted as an appendix to his lectures on Political Economy, he objects to the over-simplified formulation of the quantity theory, employed in the reasoning of the *Bullion Report*, and stresses the more "indirect connection between the high prices and an increased circulating medium." He quotes first a statement from a letter by Lord Lauderdale that

"*By the same act* with which a bank increases the circulating medium of a country, it issues into the community a mass of fictitious capital, which serves not only as circulating medium but creates an additional quantity of capital to be employed in every mode in which capital can be employed," and then adds : "The explanation you have given of the process by which this affects the price of commodities, coincides so exactly with my own ideas that it would be quite superfluous for me to follow out the speculation any farther. The radical evil, in short, seems to be, not the mere over-issue of notes, considered as an addition to our currency, but the anomalous and unchecked extension of *credit* and its inevitable effect in producing a sudden augmentation of prices by a sudden augmentation of demand. The enlarged issue deserves attention, chiefly as affording a scale for measuring how far this extension has been carried. The same degree of credit, if it could have been given without the intervention of paper currency, would have operated in exactly the same way upon prices, and upon everything else." (p. 440.)

Stewart then discusses some different opinions stated by Thornton, in the *Bullion Report*, and by Huskisson, and

[1] Lord Lauderdale had discussed the danger of a " forcible conversion of revenue into capital " or a " forced increase of capital," although in a slightly different context, already in 1804 in his *Inquiry into the Nature and Origin of Public Wealth*, pp. 262, 267/8.

proceeds to draw a conclusion which, in a curious way, anticipates the subject, and even the formulation, of a well-known recent controversy :[1]

" I have dwelt the longer on this particular view of the subject, considered in contrast with that adopted by Mr. Thornton (and apparently sanctioned in the last passage quoted from the *Bullion Report*) because the two opinions lead obviously to two very different conclusions concerning the nature of the remedy suited to the disorder. The one opinion suggests the propriety of limiting credit through the medium of a restricted currency ; the other of limiting the currency through the medium of a well regulated and discriminating credit. If the radical evil were merely an excess of the circulating medium, operating as such without the combination of any other cause, it would follow that a reduction of this quantity, by whatsoever means it were to be brought about, and however violent the effects which it might threaten, would be the only measure competent to the attainment of the end. But if, on the other hand, this excess be only symptomatic of another malady, with which, from particular circumstances, it happens to be co-existent (of an extension of credit, to wit, calculated to derange the pre-existing relations of demand and supply) then in that case the restriction and *regulation* of this credit, ought to be regarded as the primary object, and the reduction of our circulating medium attended to solely as an indication that the cure is progressive " (p. 443).

Stewart adds that, in his opinion, a repeal or relaxation of the anti-usurious laws " would go to the root of the mischief by a process more effectual, and at the same time more gentle and manageable in its operation, than an̰y other that I can imagine," and quotes in

[1] Cf. J. M. Keynes, *A Tract on Monetary Reform*, London, 1923, p. 184, and Prof. Edwin Cannan's article Limitation of Currency or Limitation of Credit, *Economic Journal*, Vol. 34, 1924, reprinted in the author's *An Economist's Protest*, London, 1927.

corroboration of that view the passage from Thornton in which this author anticipated Wicksell's theory as to the effect of a money rate of interest which is below the " natural " rate.[1] A little later, Stewart comes back to this point, insisting that " the *primary* cause of the depreciation is the artificial cheapness in the rate at which, in consequence of the laws against usury, the use of money may be obtained " (p. 447). And before he concludes this letter (which was written in March, 1811) he mentions that he has just seen the article (by Malthus) in the *Edinburgh Review* of February and that he was agreeably surprised to find the passage to which I have already alluded, which he quotes in full (pp. 448–449).

After all this, there can be little doubt that the theory of " forced saving " was fairly widely known among monetary writers in the early nineteenth century ; and I should not be surprised if a closer study of the literature of the time revealed still more discussions of the problem.[2] Indeed, Prof. A. M. Marget has noted a rather general allusion to it in R. Torrens' *Essay on the Production of Wealth*.[3] But

---

[1] Henry Thornton, l.c. p. 287. The passage is quoted and discussed in my *Prices and Production*, pp. 12, 13.

[2] Since these lines were first published, Professor J. Viner (*Studies in the Theory of International Trade*, 1937, pp. 189–196) has given an even more extensive list of such further early discussions of the problem than I should have expected. His main additional references are : R. Torrens, *Essay on Money and Paper Currency*, 1812, pp. 34 ff. ; T. R. Malthus, review of Tooke, *Quarterly Review*, Vol. XXIX, 1823, p. 239 ; Lord Lauderdale, *Further Considerations on the State of the Currency*, 1813, pp. 96–97 ; J. Rooke, *A Supplement to the Remarks on the Nature and Operations of Money*, 1819, pp. 68–69 ; T. Tooke, *Considerations on the State of the Currency*, 2nd Ed. 1826, pp. 23–24 ; T. Joplin, *An Illustration of Mr. Joplin's Views on Currency*, 1825, pp. 28 ff., and *Views on the Currency*, 1828, p. 146.

[3] Robert Torrens, *An Essay on the Production of Wealth*, London,

it would be surprising if an idea, which was discussed as widely as this one was, should in the course of time be entirely forgotten ; and this was by no means the case here. John Stuart Mill in the fourth of his *Essays on Some Unsettled Questions of Political Economy*—" On Profits and Interest "—written in 1829 or 1830, goes at least so far as to mention that, as a result of the activity of bankers, " revenue " may be " converted into capital ; and thus, strange as it may appear, the depreciation of the currency, when effected in this way, operates to a certain extent as a forced accumulation."[1] But he believed then that this phenomenon belonged to the " further anomalies of the rate of interest which have not, so far as we are aware, been hitherto brought within the pale of exact science."[2] The early editions of his *Principles* seem to contain nothing on this point. But in 1865, in the sixth edition, he added to his chapter on " Credit as a Substitute for Money " a footnote which so closely resembles the statement by Malthus that it seems very probable that something— perhaps the publication of D. Stewart's *Collected Works*, in 1855, containing the discussion to which we have already referred (including the quotation from Malthus)—had directed his attention to the earlier discussion of the point.

The footnote, which qualifies a statement made in

1821, p. 326 *et seq*. The reference is given by Prof. A. W. Marget in his excellent article on Léon Walras and the " Cash Balance Approach " to the Problem of the Value of Money, *Journal of Political Economy*, Vol. 39, No. 5 (October, 1931), p. 598.

[1] John Stuart Mill, *Essays on Some Unsettled Questions of Political Economy*, 2nd Ed., London, 1874, p. 118. I owe this reference to Mr. Victor Edelberg.

[2] *Ibid.*, p. 114.

the text that credit serves only to transfer capital from one person to another, is as follows :—

" To make the proposition in the text strictly true, a corrective—though a very slight one—requires to be made. The circulating medium existing in a country at a given time is partly employed in purchases for productive, partly for unproductive, consumption. According as a larger proportion of it is employed in the one way or in the other, the real capital of the country is greater or less. If, then, an addition were made to the circulating medium in the hands of unproductive consumers exclusively, a larger portion of the existing stock of commodities would be bought for unproductive consumption, and a smaller for a productive, which state of things, while it lasted, would be equivalent to a diminution of capital ; and, on the contrary, if the addition made be to the portion of the circulating medium which is in the hands of producers, and destined for their business, a greater portion of the commodities of the country will be, for the present, employed as capital, and a less portion unproductively. Now an effect of this latter character naturally attends some extensions of credit, especially when taking place in the form of bank notes or other instruments of exchange. The additional bank notes are, in ordinary course, first issued to producers or dealers, to be employed as capital ; and though the stock of commodities in the country is no greater than before, yet as a greater share of that stock now comes by purchase into the hands of producers and dealers, to that extent what would have been unproductively consumed is applied to production, and there is a real increase of capital. The effect ceases, and a counter-process takes place, when the additional credit is stopped, and the notes called in."[1]

Only fourteen years after this remarkably clear state-

---

[1] J. S. Mill, *Principles of Political Economy*, Ed. Ashley, p. 512. This passage in the Principles has been pointed out by Prof. Marco Fanno in his article " Cicli di produzione, cicli di credito e fluttuazioni industriali," *Giornali degli Economisti*, Mai, 1931, p. 31 of the reprint.

ment by John Stuart Mill, we find that exposition of the theory of " forced saving " to which the modern developments can be pretty definitely traced. Whether Léon Walras, who in 1879 devoted a long section of his *Théorie Mathématique du Billet de Banque* to a discussion of it, had been directly influenced by Mill is not known ; but it seems quite probable. That Walras inspired K. Wicksell and, through Wicksell, all the later German authors who dealt with the problem, there can be little doubt. But Walras' very interesting discussion was practically forgotten, until attention was recently drawn to it by Professor Marget in the article quoted above. Indeed, Walras there gives more than his disciple Wicksell—or any other author up to quite recent times. In a section headed " Accroissement du Capital par l'émission des Billets de Banque," he analyses, in great detail, what he calls the undeniable fact that " L'émission des billets de banque pour une certaine somme permet une augmentation dans la quantité du capital pour une somme égale."[1] He sees clearly that the expansion of bank credit " crée non pas un capital nouveau, mais une demande nouvelle de capital, et le capital lui-même reste à créer " ; in consequence, " la proportion de la production des revenues consommables et des capitaux neufs est changée, il y a diminution dans la quantité des uns et augmentation dans la quantité des autres." The situation is not quite the same as in the case of a sudden and considerable increase in saving, because

" dans le cas de l'émission des billets de banque, comme cela aurait aussi lieu dans le cas de la découverte de

[1] Cf. Léon Walras, *Études d'Économie Politique Appliquée*, Lausanne and Paris, 1898, pp. 348–356.

monnaie métallique, il y a augmentation de demande d'un côté sans diminution de demande de l'autre, et, par suite, augmentation dans la valeur totale de la production. Ainsi : *L'émission de billets de banque pour une certaine somme amère, pendant toute la période d'émission, une hausse du prix des produits consistant en revenus consommables et capitaux neufs qui se mesure approximativement par le rapport du montant de l'émission au montant du revenu social antérieur.* Ce phénomène est transitoire une fois l'émission terminée, la hausse en question disparait, et il ne subsiste plus que celle provenant de la dépréciation du métal précieux."

Finally, Walras elaborates this theory in algebraic form and gives an arithmetical example in order to show what the practical importance of the phenomenon may be.

In Wicksell's exposition,[1] this idea, although only briefly mentioned, becomes an integral part of his theory as to the effect of a money rate of interest which is different from the equilibrium rate. From Wicksell, the idea was taken over by Mises,[2] who elaborated it still further, and from Mises by Schumpeter.[3] Through their influence, it has recently become quite a familiar feature of German writings on the subject,[4] even before the interest in these problems was further stimulated by the new, and apparently independent, development of similar ideas among the Cambridge School of Economists. Mr. D. H. Robertson's " Imposed

---

[1] Knut Wicksell, *Geldzins und Güterpreise*, Jena, 1898, pp. 103, 142.

[2] L. v. Mises, *Theorie des Geldes und der Umlaufsmittel*, München, 1912.

[3] Josef Schumpeter, *Theorie der wirtschaftlichen Entwicklung*, Leipzig, 1912.

[4] These more recent German developments have been discussed, in some detail, in an article by Dr. Erich Egner, " Zur Lehre vom Zwangssparen," *Zeitschrift für die gesamte Staatswissenschaft*, 1928.

Lacking " and Professor Pigou's " Forced Levies " are, of course, just the same thing as Bentham's " Forced Frugality," J. S. Mill's " Forced Accumulation " and the " Erzwungene Sparen " or " Zwangssparen " of Wicksell and the German authors. Mr. J. M. Keynes, however, who discusses the same problem in his *Treatise on Money*,[1] rejects this terminology and prefers to speak simply of investment being in excess of saving ; and there is much to be said in favour of this. Unfortunately, however, Mr. Keynes uses the terms " saving " and " investing " in a sense quite different from the usual one, so that, for some time, the danger of confusion may make difficult the acceptance of what is perhaps the better terminology.

[1] i, 171.

APPENDIX

THE " PARADOX " OF SAVING[1]

I

THE assertion that saving renders the purchasing power of the consumer insufficient to take up the volume of current production, although made more often by members of the lay public than by professional economists, is almost as old as the science of political economy itself. The question of the utility of " unproductive " expenditure was first raised by the Mercantilists, who were thinking chiefly of luxury expenditure.

The idea recurs in those writings of Lauderdale and Malthus which gave rise to the celebrated *Théorie des Débouchés* of James Mill and J. B. Say, and, in spite of many attempts to refute it, it permeates the main doctrines of Socialist economics right up to T. Veblen, and Mr. J. A. Hobson.

But while in this way the idea has found a greater popularity in quasi-scientific and propagandist literature than perhaps any other economic doctrine hitherto, fortunately it has not succeeded as yet in depriving

[1] The following is a translation of an essay, which originally appeared in the *Zeitschrift für Nationalökonomie*, Bd. I, Heft III, 1929, under the title " Gibt es einen Widersinn des Sparens ? " The translation is the work of Mr. Nicholas Kaldor and Dr. Georg Tugendhat and was first published in *Economica*, May, 1931. It is now reprinted with some minor textual revisions.

saving of its general respectability, and we have yet to learn that any of the numerous monetary measures intended to counteract its supposedly harmful effects have been put into practice. On the contrary, we have recently witnessed the edifying spectacle of a " World Saving Day," on which central bank governors and ministers of finance vied with each other in attempting to disseminate the virtue of saving as widely as possible throughout their respective nations. And even though there are those who demand an increase in the currency on the grounds that there is an increased tendency to save, it is hard to believe that the presidents of central banks at any rate will prove very ready listeners.

This state of affairs, however, may yet be endangered by a new theory of under-consumption now current in the United States and in England. Its authors are people who spare neither money nor time in the propagation of their ideas. Their doctrine is no less fallacious than all the previous theories of under-consumption, but it is not impossible that with able exposition and extensive financial backing it may exert a certain influence on policy in Anglo-Saxon countries. For this reason it seems worth while subjecting this theory to detailed and exhaustive criticism.

II

The teachings of Messrs. Foster and Catchings, with which I am primarily concerned in this study, attained their widest circulation in the United States where they have achieved considerable repute not only among members of the public, but also among professional economists. To understand this success it is necessary to know something of the background of the theory and the very able means by which it has been and still is being propagated. Quite apart from its analytical significance, for European observers at any rate the story has a certain spectacular interest. I propose, therefore, to deal with it at some length.

Let us start with the two authors. The history of their joint careers provides certain points which give a clue to the origin of their teaching. Waddill Catchings was born in the south ; he had a successful career as a lawyer and banker, finally reaching a high position in the iron and steel industry. In 1920 he, and a number of fellow-students from Harvard, decided to commemorate a deceased friend. For this purpose they founded the " Pollak Foundation for Economic Research." They appointed as director another Harvard friend, William Trufant Foster, a pedagogue, at one time a college president. The Foundation had an annual income of $25,000 and it soon began to be responsible for the publication of important books on economic subjects, some of them by well-known economists, such as Irving Fisher's *Making of Index-Numbers*, others by members of the Foundation, such as A. B. Hasting's *Costs and Profits*, and, above all, *Money* by Messrs. Foster and Catchings themselves. In this latter work, although it is primarily a very able and instructive exposition of the theory of money, the authors laid the basis of their theory of trade depression later to be fully expounded in their work on *Profits*. In *Money*, they emphasise especially those parts dealing with the circulation of money and the effects on markets of changes in the rate of flow of money. After describing how circulation starts from the market for consumption goods, from which it passes into the market for production goods, and finally returns to its original source, they discuss the conditions under which this process creates a steady demand for the goods offered for sale, and the factors which influence the circulation of money either by accelerating or retarding it. While, in a barter economy, supply and demand are necessarily identical, the appearance of money is shown to be capable of disturbing this equilibrium, since it is only possible to maintain production at the existing level if the producers spend money at the same rate as that at which they receive it. Thus the circulation of money between the various stages of the economic process becomes the central problem of all investigation, not only of changes in the value of money, but also of the influences affecting cyclical fluctuations.

Indeed they even go so far as to lay it down that : " Money spent in the consumption of commodities is the force that moves all the wheels of industry. When this force remains in the right relation to the volume of commodities offered for sale, business proceeds steadily. When money is spent faster than the commodities reach the retail markets, business booms forward. When commodities continue to reach the retail markets faster than money is spent, business slackens. To move commodities year after year without disturbing business, enough money must be spent by consumers, and no more than enough, to match all the commodities, dollar for dollar."[1]

[1] W. T. Foster and W. Catchings : *Money*. Publications of the Pollak Foundation for Economic Research, No. 2, Boston and New York, Houghton Mifflin, 1923 (p. 277). (A third edition was published in 1928.)

It is this theory which forms the basis of the trade cycle theory, which is set forth in great detail in *Profits*,[1] published three years later.   In this voluminous work, with which we shall be concerned in the next sections, Messrs. Foster and Catchings give the most elaborate and careful exposition of their theory.   But, despite the clear and entertaining exposition, it failed to secure for the theory the wide circulation desired by its authors. They proceeded, therefore, to restate the main principles in popular language, first in their *Business without a Buyer*,[2] and later in abridged form in an essay in the *Atlantic Monthly*, which was distributed freely as a reprint in hundreds of thousands of copies.[3]   Most effective, however, in advertising their ideas was the peculiar competition held in connection with the publication of *Profits*.   By offering a prize of $5,000 for the best adverse criticism of the theory contained in this work, the promoters invited the whole world to refute them.   But before dealing with the results of this competition it is necessary to consider the general principles of their work.

[1] W. T. Foster and W. Catchings :   *Profits*, Publications of the Pollak Foundation, No. 8, Boston and New York, Houghton Mifflin, 1925.

[2] W. T. Foster and W. Catchings :   *Business without a Buyer*, Pollak Foundation, Boston and New York, Houghton Mifflin, 1927, second revised edition, No. 10, 1928.

[3] W. T. Foster and W. Catchings :   *The Dilemma of Thrift*, reprinted from an article in the *Atlantic Monthly* under the title : " Progress and Plenty, a Way out of the Dilemma of Thrift " ; together with another article published in the *Century Magazine*.   The pamphlet was published by the Pollak · Foundation (Newton 58, Mass., U.S.A.) which supplies copies free on request.

III

The theory of crises advanced by Messrs. Foster and Catchings in *Profits* is preceded by a detailed explanation of the organisation of the present economic structure. This justification of the existing " Money and Profit System," as it is called by the authors, fills about one-half of the volume of four hundred pages. For our purpose, it is sufficient to mention that in this part the function of entrepreneur's profit as a factor determining the direction and extent of production is investigated ; but it is worth remarking even at this juncture that the authors succeed in completing this investigation without at any point making clear the real function of capital as a factor of production. Our main concern in this article, however, is confined to the fifth and last part of *Profits* which deals with " Money and Profits in Relation to Consumption," and which, according to the authors themselves, represents a more or less independent object for critical study.[1] It will be necessary in this connection also to refer in some detail to the short essay entitled *The Dilemma of Thrift*.

The main thesis of the book is stated as follows : " The one thing that is needed above all others to sustain a forward movement of business is enough money in the hands of consumers."[2] Now in the present state of affairs a situation arises from time to time when the buying power in the hands of the consumers is insufficient to purchase the whole industrial

---

[1] Cf. Pollak *Prize Essays*, criticism of *Profits*, a book by W. T. Foster and W. Catchings, Pollak Foundation, Newton, 1927.

[2] *Profits*, p. 11.

output at prices which cover costs. The consequent diminution in sales in the market for consumption goods results in unemployment of factories and plant, that is to say, in crises and trade depressions. The question is : Where does the deficit in the consumers' income originate ? The earlier exposition in *Money* and *Profits* affords no explanation of this phenomenon, since it does not take into account the three principle factors upon which the velocity of circulation, and therefore the " annual production-consumption equation " depend : *i.e.*, the influence of saving, of profits, and of changes in the volume of currency. The most important of these factors is saving, both individual and corporate. To elucidate this point the authors proceed to examine a series of numerical examples and, in the course of this examination, they introduce a number of fictitious assumptions, which, as we shall see later, have an important bearing upon their conclusions. They assume, that by a process of vertical and horizontal integration, the whole industry of the isolated country considered has been united into one single enterprise, payments from which in the form of wages, dividends and salaries form the only source of the community's income. (There are no taxes or Government expenditure of any kind.) It is assumed further that the price-level, the volume of currency and the velocity of circulation remain constant, and that wages are received and spent during the same economic period in which the goods are manufactured, while these goods are only sold in the following period, and the profits earned on them are also distributed and spent by the recipients during this same period.[1]

[1] Op. cit., 268.

206 PROFITS, INTEREST AND INVESTMENT

With the aid of numerical examples of this sort, the authors demonstrate that, under these conditions, there can be no difficulty in selling the goods manufactured, either in the case of a constant volume of production or of a rising volume per wage-unit, so long as " industry continues to return to consumers in some way all the money that it took from consumers in the sales price of its product, and as long as consumers spend all that they receive."[1] But as soon as the company retains part of the profits in the business, not for the purpose of carrying larger stocks, financing the sale of an increased product, or in *unsuccessful* attempts to improve equipment—for these things are comparatively harmless—but in order to improve " capital facilities," which puts it in the position to increase the volume of production, this happy state of affairs changes. As soon as the increased volume of products reaches the market, it is inevitable that the means of payment in the hands of the consumer should prove insufficient to take up the product at remunerative prices. So long as the process of investment is going on no difficulty arises, since the rise in the total wage bill resulting from the increased number of workmen necessary to carry out the extension equals the loss in the shareholders' income resulting from the reduction in dividends, and thus the relation between the volume of production and the money spent on it remains unaltered. The crisis sets in with the appearance on the market of the surplus output. The money in the hands of the consumer does not increase any further (the sums necessary for the extension of production

[1] Op. cit., p. 273.

having already been spent by the wage-earners in the previous period to take up the smaller volume) and, since it is assumed that there is no fall in prices, a proportion of the enlarged product must therefore remain unsold.

In *The Dilemma of Thrift*, Messrs. Foster and Catchings provide the following description of the events leading up to this crisis[1] : " Suppose, however, it (the corporation) uses the remaining one million dollars of profits to build additional cars, in such a way that all this money goes directly or indirectly to consumers. The company has now disbursed exactly enough money to cover the full sales-price of the cars it has already marketed ; but where are the consumers to obtain enough money to buy the additional cars ? The corporation has given them nothing with which to buy these cars." The new cars, therefore, must remain unsold, " unless the deficiency (in consumers' income) is made up from outside sources."[2]

According to Messrs. Foster and Catchings the significant difference between the money spent upon consumption goods and money invested rests upon the fact that money of the former kind is " used *first* to take away consumers' goods, whereas in many cases money invested is used *first* to produce more consumers' goods."[3] " Money that is once used to bring about the production of goods is again used to bring about the

---

[1] *Dilemma of Thrift*, p. 15.

[2] *Profits*, p. 281, where the following remark is appended to that qualification : " We here make that qualification, once and for all, with respect to every case in this and the following chapters," which later gave the authors' critics an opportunity to accuse them (*Prize Essays*, p. 12) of a misunderstanding of the main point of their argument.

[3] *Profits*, p. 284.

production of goods, before it is used to bring about the consumption of goods. In other words, it is used twice in succession to create supply ; whereas if the $100,000 in question, instead of having been *invested* in the production of additional goods, had been paid out as dividends and *spent* by the recipients, the $100,000 would have been used alternately to bring goods to the markets and to take goods off the markets."[1] Statements of this sort, which are repeatedly used by the authors, have led so acute a thinker as Mr. D. H. Robertson to remark that he could not attach any sense to them whatever.[2] It therefore seems worth while attempting to restate this part of the theory in more familiar language. Granting the initial presuppositions of the authors it is, I think, unassailable. So long as the total disbursements during the course of production are spent on consumption goods, the expenses of production are necessarily equal to the proceeds of the sale of the goods purchased. If, however, certain amounts, such as interest earned on capital, or profit, which could be spent on consumption goods without reducing the existing capital stock, are applied to purchasing additional means of production, the sum total spent on production rises without being accompanied by an equivalent increase in the sums available to buy the final product. It is in this " short-circuit " in the circulation of money, as Mr. P. W. Martin,[3] whose

[1] *Profits*, p. 279.
[2] D. H. Robertson : "The Monetary Doctrines of Messrs. Foster and Catchings," *Quarterly Journal of Economics*, Vol. XLIII, p. 483, May, 1929.
[3] P. W. Martin : *The Flaw in the Price System*, London, 1924 ; *The Limited Market*, London, 1926, and *Unemployment and Purchasing Power*, London, 1929.

ideas are closely related to those of Messrs. Foster and
Catchings, describes it, that we find the alleged cause
of the deficiency in the buying power of the consumer.

Now since the results of corporate saving and of
individual saving must be alike, since individuals as
well as corporations must save if they are to progress,
but since, if this theory is correct, they cannot save at
present without frustrating to a certain extent the
social purpose of saving, the *Dilemma of Thrift* is
unescapable. " From the standpoint of society, therefore, it is impossible to save intelligently without first
solving the problem of adequate consumer income.
As it is to-day, certain individuals can save at the
expense of other individuals ; certain corporations can
save at the expense of other corporations ; and, from
the standpoint of the individual and of the corporation,
these savings are real. But society as a whole cannot
save anything worth saving at the expense of consumers as a whole, for the capacity of consumers to
benefit by what is saved is the sole test of its worth."[1]

After the main thesis of the theory has thus been
expounded the authors drop a number of artificial
assumptions, and attempt to bring the theory nearer
to reality. The first assumption to be abandoned is
that of a stable price-level (this assumption, by the way,
was never consistent with their other assumptions).
They then examine the effects of falling prices, which
alone make it possible to sell the whole of the enlarged
product. But falling prices, they argue, make it impossible for industry to maintain production at the new
level. The fall of prices causes profits to disappear, and

---

[1] *Profits*, p. 294.

with profits every incentive to the continuation of production.[1] Moreover, it is argued, it is a matter of experience that falling prices render an extension of production impossible. " If there is any fact concerning which our statistical evidence fully supports our reasoning, it is the fact that falling prices put a damper on productive activity."[2] Only on paper is it possible, in spite of falling prices, to carry out productive extensions by means of falling costs, because only on paper can you regulate the diminution of cost so that even the enlarged product can be sold with sufficient profits. In the existing economic system, with the many independent units composing it, such a development is not to be expected. On the contrary, we should rather expect price movements in the wrong direction. A fall in the price of consumption goods, therefore, must always bring about a diminution of production.[3]

Having thus attempted to show that a general fall in prices can never bring about a solution of the problem, the authors next proceed to consider *changes in the volume of money*. After all that has been said, it is argued, it should be clear that even changes in the volume of money can only solve the problem in so far as they influence the " production-consumption equation." " It is not sufficient for this purpose that the total volume of money be increased. The money must go into circulation in such a way that the flow of new money into the hands of the consumers is equal in value, at the current retail price-level, to the flow of new goods into consumers' markets. The question

[1] Op. cit., p. 299.
[2] Op. cit., p. 302.
[3] Op. cit., pp. 302–13.

is not, then, whether currency or bank-credit, or both, should be increased year after year, but in what way the new money should be introduced into the circuit flow."[1]

Now unhappily, under the existing system of money and credit, additional money gets into circulation, not on the side of the consumers but on the side of the producers, and thus only aggravates the evil of the discrepancy between producers' disbursements and consumers' money expenditure. Moreover, this system of increasing the money supply through productive credits has the further effect that additions to the money supply take place when they are least necessary. The extension of production which they finance is a response to a lively demand. But when a falling off of consumers' demand is noticeable then credit is restricted and the trouble is aggravated. Thus the modern claim to restrict credit at the first sign of increasing warehouse stocks, and vice versa, is thoroughly pernicious. " In this way . . . every advance towards higher standards of living would promptly be checked ; for whenever it appeared that consumer income was too small, it would be made smaller still through wage reductions, and under-production would follow promptly."[2] Nevertheless, it would be easy to arrange an increase in consumers' credits, and it is only in this way that the deficiency in the purchasing power of the consumer, and thus the cause of the depression, can be removed. " Theoretically, then, it is always possible to add to the money circulation in such a way as to benefit the community. . . . In any conceivable

---

[1] Op. cit., p. 307.
[2] *Profits*, p. 324.

situation . . . an all-wise despot could make a net gain to the community by increasing the volume of money in circulation. . . . If any safe and practicable means could be devised, in connection with increased public works and decreased taxes, or in any other connection, of issuing just enough money to consumers to provide for individual savings and to enable them to buy an enlarged output, and business men were confident that issues to consumers would continue at this rate and at no other rate, there would be no drop in the price-level and no reason for curtailing production, but, on the contrary, the most powerful incentive for increasing production."[1]

In *Profits*, the authors do not go further than to hint at these proposals. After a not very successful attempt at statistical verification they conclude that, under the present order of things, every attempt at increasing production must be checked by the fact that the demand of the consumer cannot keep pace with the supply. To remove the causes of this under-consumption is one of the most promising and most urgent problems for the present generation. " Indeed, it is doubtful whether any other way of helping humanity holds out such large immediate possibilities."[2]

But before such reforms can be achieved professional economists will have to admit the inadequacy of their present theories. " If the main contentions of *Money* and *Profits* are sound, much of our traditional economic teaching is unsound, and overlooks some of the fundamentals which must be better understood before it

[1] Op. cit., pp. 330–1.
[2] *Profits*, p. 417.

will be possible to solve the economic problem."[1]
Conversion of professional economists was therefore
the main purpose of the campaign which was launched
by offering a prize for the best adverse criticism of
Profits.

IV

The result of this competition for the best adverse
criticism of their theory was the most remarkable
success achieved by Messrs. Foster and Catchings. The
three members of the jury, Professor Wesley C. Mitchell,
the late Allyn A. Young, and Mr. Owen D. Young,
the President of the General Electric Company, of
" Young Plan " fame, had no less than four hundred
and thirty-five essays to examine. In the introduction
to the little volume in which the prize essay and others
were published,[2] Messrs. Foster and Catchings relate,
with some pride, that at least fifty universities, forty-
two American States, and twenty-five foreign countries
were represented. Among the authors were at least
forty authors of books on economics, fifty professors of
political economy, sixty accounting experts, bankers,
editors, statisticians, directors of large companies, etc.—
among them " some of the ablest men in the Federal
Reserve System," a functionary of the American
Economic Association, a former President of that

---

[1] Op. cit., p. 416.
[2] *Pollak Prize Essays: Criticisms of " Profits,"* a book by
W. T. Foster and W. Catchings. Essays by R. W. Souter, Frederick
Law Olmsted, C. F. Bickerdike, Victor Valentinovitch Novogilov.
Newton, Mass., 1927. Cf. also the introduction to *Business without
a Buyer*.

Society, and "several of the most highly-reputed economists in the British Empire."

But despite this highly respectable mass-attack of adverse criticism, Messrs. Foster and Catchings remained convinced that their theory still held its own. Moreover, they were able to quote the opinion of one of the umpires,[1] that notwithstanding all that had been said against it, the substance of the theory remained untouched. This sounds extraordinary. But what is more extraordinary is that a candid perusal of the various criticisms which have been published forces one to admit that it is true. So far, the main theory, and what in my opinion is the fundamental misconception of Messrs. Foster and Catchings, has remained unanswered. The meritorious and readable works which were published in the *Prize Essays*, equally with criticisms published elsewhere,[2] direct their criticism only against details. They accept the main thesis of Messrs. Foster and Catchings. Only the two essays of Novogilov and Adams, which we shall have occasion to mention later on, touch upon the critical points, and even here they do not make their respective objections the basic part of their criticism, or develop them into an independent refutation.

In the case of Novogilov's work, it is possible that

---

[1] Op. cit., p. 6. See also the introduction to *Business without a Buyer*.

[2] To be mentioned especially are : A. B. Adams, *Profits, Progress and Prosperity*, New York, 1927 ; A. H. Hansen, *Business Cycle Theory, its Development and Present Status*, Boston, New York, 1927 (a prize essay published separately) ; H. Neisser, *Theorie des wirtschaftlichen Gleichgewichtes, Kölner sozialpolitische Vierteljahrschrift*, Vol. VI., 1927, especially pp. 124-35 ; D. H. Robertson, "The Monetary Doctrines of Messrs. Foster and Catchings," *Quarterly Journal of Economics*, Vol. XLIII, No. 3, May, 1929.

this is an injustice. In the *Prize Essays* it was only
published in abridged form, and just the part dealing
with the influence of varying quantities of product at
the various stages of production on the level of profits
was entirely left out.[1] It is to be hoped that one day it
will be published in its entirety. Mr. A. B. Adams'
essay, on the other hand, whose criticism on many points
coincides with that developed in this essay, and which
in an incidental remark foreshadows one of its main
theses,[2] suffers from the fact that the author himself
does not realise the full importance of his objections,
and therefore only criticises the application of Messrs.
Foster and Catchings' theory to the case of investment
in fixed capital, while admitting its correctness in the
case of investment in circulating capital. But even Mr.
Adams seems insufficiently to appreciate the function
of capital and the conditions determining its utilisation
—a deficiency which is common both to the authors of
the theory and to all their critics.

As for the rest, they all endeavour to prove that the
existing currency organisation suffices to increase the
supply of money in the course of an extension of
production so as to avoid a fall in the price-level. Some
of them also point out that the extension of production
can also bring about a diminution in costs per unit,
so that falling prices need not always put a damper
on production. But the alleged necessity to ease the
sale of the enlarged product by an increase in the
money supply is, in general, allowed to pass
unquestioned. In doing this, however, the critics place
themselves in a difficult position. For the contention of

[1] Cf. *Prize Essays*, pp. 118–24.
[2] See below, p. 251.

Messrs. Foster and Catchings that productive credits aggravate still more the deficiency in the purchasing power of the consumer is clearly a corollary of the fundamental concept on which the claim for increasing the volume of money by productive extensions is based. To meet this difficulty the critics resort to various expedients. Some make very ingenious investigations into the order of succession of various money movements. Some attempt to refute the rather shaky assumptions in regard to the formation of profits in the course of productive extensions. Correct as these objections may be, they miss the point. The main thesis remains untouched.

V

It is clear that this is the opinion of Messrs. Foster and Catchings, for in their *Business without a Buyer*, published after the close of the prize competition, they do not make any significant alterations in the exposition of their theory. Fortified by the result of the competition, they then proceeded to develop the practical consequences of their theory. In *The Road to Plenty*,[1] which embodies the results of these further reflections, they make no attempt to appeal to economists. Despite the extremely favourable reception of their former books, it appears they are far from satisfied with professional economists. Both in the introduction to the

---

[1] W. T. Foster and W. Catchings : *The Road to Plenty* (Publications of Pollak Foundation, No. 11), Boston and New York, Houghton Mifflin, 1928 ; second edition, revised, 1928. A popular edition of 50,000 copies of the *Road to Plenty* was published and sold (230 pp., in full cloth binding) for 25 cents !

Prize Essays and in *Business without a Buyer* they
dwelt with some sprightliness on the lack of enlighten-
ment in such circles.   Now they turn to the general
public and cast their theory in the form of a novel.   The
book records a conversation in the smoking compart-
ment of a train where the complaints of a warm-hearted
friend of humanity cause a genial business man to
explain the causes of crises and unemployment
according to the theory of the authors, and then to
defend the latter against the objections of a solicitor
and a professor of economics (who, of course, comes out
worst).   Finally, all those present (including a member
of the House of Representatives) are roused to a great
pitch of enthusiasm about the concrete proposals based
upon it.

These proposals are formulated still more clearly in
a further essay, *Progress and Plenty*,[1] and before
proceeding to examine the theory it is worth while
setting them forth explicitly.   The first demand of the
authors, and the condition for the execution of their
further proposals, is an extension of business statistics
in the direction of a more exact knowledge of the sales
of consumption goods—in the first place, a complete
and reliable index of retail prices ; secondly, statistics
of all factors influencing these prices (*i.e.*, all possible
economic data).   These should be collected by public
authorities and published promptly, in order to give
information and orientation to the business world.   On

[1] W. T. Foster and W. Catchings : *Progress and Plenty, A Way
out of the Dilemma of Thrift* reprinted from the *Century Magazine*,
July, 1928. Reprinted also together with *The Dilemma of Thrift*. The
second edition of *The Road to Plenty*, which I received after writing
this article, takes over almost word for word the statements quoted
here from *Progress and Plenty*.

the basis of such statistics, all public works and all financial operations of the Government should be directed in such a way as to even out fluctuations in the demand for consumption goods. In *Progress and Plenty*,[1] Messrs. Foster and Catchings recommend the delegation of the business of collecting data, and their application to the distribution of public works to a separate body, the " Federal Budget Board." Just as the Federal Reserve Board directs a system for the financing of production, the Federal Budget Board should direct the financing of consumption and prevent disturbances of the economic system arising from consumption lagging behind production.

So far, apart from the demand for a new Board, the proposal contains nothing beyond the much-discussed plan for distributing public works in time in such a way as to concentrate all those capable of being postponed to times of depression. But Messrs. Foster and Catchings are not satisfied with this. They realise that such a plan would have undesirable effects if the necessary sums were collected and locked up in the public Treasury in times of prosperity and spent in case of need. On the other hand, to raise the money by taxation at the time when it is needed for public works would be still less likely to achieve the desired end. Only an increase in the volume of money for the purpose of consumption can solve the problem : " Progress requires a constant flow of new money to consumers. If, therefore, business indexes show the need for a

---

[1] P. 16 of the independent reprint, p. 37 of the reprint together with *The Dilemma of Thrift* (the reference to the latter will always be given in brackets below). Cf. also *The Road to Plenty*, 2nd Ed., p. 188.

reinforced consumer demand which cannot be met
without additional Government expenditure, the Board
should bring about such expenditure, not only out of
funds previously accumulated for that purpose, but
at times out of loans which involve an expansion of
bank credit. *This feature of the plan is essential.*[1] It
follows that the Government should borrow and spend
the money whenever the indexes show that the needed
flow of money will not come from other sources."[2]

As might be expected, the authors protest[3] that all
this is not to be regarded as inflationary. Before its
publication they had promised that it should contain
" nothing dangerous or even distasteful," and that it
would not involve " unlimited issues of fiat money."[4]
We shall deal critically with these proposals in the last
section of this article. At present, it need only be
remarked that even critics who sympathise with
Messrs. Foster and Catchings' theory have been unable
to conceal their scruples on this point. Mr. D. H.
Robertson[5] remarks very correctly that he has no
doubts that " they were born with a double dose of the
inflation bacillus in their composition ; and though
they have done their best to exorcise it with prayer
and fasting, so that they are able to look down with
detached pity on more gravely affected sufferers, such
as Major Douglas, yet at critical moments the bacillus
is always apt to take charge of the argument." It is,
therefore, all the more astounding that they are able

[1] My italics.
[2] *Progress and Plenty*, p. 22 (42), and almost in the same words in
The Road to Plenty, 2nd Ed., p. 193.
[3] *The Road to Plenty*, 2nd Ed., p. 209.
[4] *Prize Essays*, p. 5.
[5] Op. cit., p. 498.

to quote in the advertisements to *The Road to Plenty* (it is true without mentioning the source) the opinion of no less an authority than the late Professor A. A. Young, that " on economic grounds, the plan for prosperity " proposed in *The Road to Plenty* " is soundly conceived," and that (according to the same source) Mr. W. M. Persons should have thought the plan " practicable and important."

In wider circles, the proposals of Messrs. Foster and Catchings seem to have had an extraordinary effect. President Hoover's pledge to carry out, within practical limits, such a regulation of public works as would alleviate unemployment, has been a powerful lever to their argument. In a recent pamphlet[1] they announce that Senator Wagner from New York has already brought a Bill before Congress for creating a " Federal Unemployment Stabilisation Board " with very similar functions to their " Federal Budget Board." So far it has not been proposed that this Board should finance public works with additional bank money, and even Messrs. Foster and Catchings have guarded themselves from demanding the execution of this part of their proposals—even in connection with the Hoover Plans. Instead they have concentrated on a criticism of the policy of the Federal Reserve Board in raising its discount rate at a time of falling prices and falling employment.[2] It is pressure of this sort which constitutes a danger both in America and elsewhere if such theories gain further popularity. At this point, therefore, we may pass to a criticism of their validity.

[1] W. T. Foster and W. Catchings : *Better Jobs and More of them. The Government's Part in Preventing Unemployment.* **Reprinted** from the *Century Magazine*, July, 1929.
[2] Op. cit., p. 17.

VI

It is constantly assumed by Messrs. Foster and Catchings that the investment of savings for the extension of production necessarily increases the total costs of production by the full amount of the invested savings. This follows clearly from their continual emphasis on the " fact " that the value of the increased product is raised by the amount invested, and that therefore it can only be sold profitably for a proportionately higher sum. It is implied by the examples, in which it is always assumed that the increase in the current outlay in wages, etc., exactly corresponds with the sums invested. Now there is a certain initial obscurity in this assumption, since it is obvious that the costs of the product produced during an economic period cannot rise by the whole of the newly-invested sum if this is invested in durable instruments, but only in proportion to the depreciation of the new durable capital goods ; a fact which is not made clear in their exposition. My main objection, however, is not concerned with this circumstance—which it is impossible to believe that the authors could entirely overlook—but rather with their assumption that generally, over *any* length of time, the costs of production can increase by the whole of the newly-invested amount. This view, which is based on a complete misunderstanding of the function of capital as a " carrying " agent, assumes that the increased volume of production brought about by the new investments must be undertaken with the same methods as the smaller volume produced before the new movement took place. Such an assumption may be true for a single enterprise, but never for industry as a whole. For in industry as a whole an increase in the available supply of capital always necessitates a *change* in the methods of production in the sense of a transition to more capitalistic, more " roundabout," processes.

For in order that there may be an increase in the volume of production without a change in the methods of production, not only the available supply of capital, but also the supply of all other factors of production must be increased in similar proportion. In regard to land, at any rate, this is practically impossible. It is just as inadmissible to assume that the complementary factors which are necessary for the extension of production are previously unemployed, and find employment only with the appearance of the new savings.[1]

A correct view of the reactions on production as a whole of the investment of new savings must be envisaged in this way : At first the new savings will serve the purpose of *transferring a portion of the original means of production previously employed in producing consumers' goods to the production of new producers' goods*. The supply of consumers' goods must, therefore,

---

[1] Messrs. Foster and Catchings seem to avail themselves of the assumption of an " industrial reserve army "—a notion much favoured in trade cycle theory—from which the labour power necessary for a proportional extension of production can always be obtained at will. Quite apart from the incompatibility of this assumption with the known facts, it is theoretically inadmissible as a starting-point for a theory which attempts, like Messrs. Foster and Catchings, to show the causes of crises, and thus of unemployment, on the basis of the modern " equilibrium theory " of price-determination. Only on the basis of an economic theory which, like the Marxian, tries to explain the existence of *permanent* unemployment of considerable proportions independently of crises would such an assumption be theoretically permissible.

temporarily fall off as an immediate consequence of the investment of new savings (a circumstance constantly overlooked by Messrs. Foster and Catchings).[1]   No unfavourable effects on the sales of consumption goods follow from this, for the demand for consumption goods and the amount of original means of production employed in producing them decrease in similar proportions. And indeed even Messrs. Foster and Catchings do not make any such assertion.   Their difficulties begin only at the moment when the increased volume of consumption goods, brought about by the new investment, comes on to the market.

Now this increase in the volume of consumption goods can only be effected through an increase in the volume of capital employed in production.   Such capital, once it has been brought into existence, does not maintain itself automatically.   This increase makes it necessary that, henceforward, a greater proportion of the existing means of production should be permanently devoted to the production of capital goods, and a smaller part to finishing consumption goods ;   and this shift in the immediate utilisation of means of production must, under the conditions prevailing in the modern economic system, conform with a change in the relative amount of money expended in the various stages of production. But this question of the relation between the sums of money expended in any period on consumption goods on the one hand and on production goods on

---

[1] Novogilov, who—as far as I can see—is the only critic who emphasises this circumstance (p. 120, op. cit.), puts a favourable interpretation on the exposition in *Profits*, namely that the authors assume that " the population as a whole must increase its expenditure of labour, but consume not more than in the first years " (p. 108). But how should savings occasion an increased expenditure of labour ?

the other, brings us to the fundamental flaw in Messrs. Foster and Catchings' theory.

VII

Messrs. Foster and Catchings base the whole of their exposition on an hypothesis of what may be called single-stage production, in which, in a state of equilibrium the money received in every period from the sale of consumption goods must equal the amount of money expended on all kinds of production goods in the same period.[1] Hence they are incapable of conceiving an extension of production save, so to speak, in the " width "—an extension involving the expenditure of the new savings side by side with the sums which were already being spent on the ultimate factors of production, this is to say, the recipients of net income. It is easy to see how they arrive at this position. They assume a single enterprise in which all goods are produced from beginning to end (there will be much to say about this later), and because of this they entirely overlook the phenomenon of changes to more or less capitalistic methods of production.

Let us for the time being avoid this assumption, and

[1] This conception, which is completely erroneous at any rate as far as it applies to a modern economic system, is very often met in economic literature, and may be traced back as far as Adam Smith, who wrote (*Wealth of Nations*, Ed. Cannan, Vol. I, p. 305) : " The value of the goods circulated between the different dealers never can exceed the value of those circulated between dealers and consumers ; whatever is bought by the dealer being ultimately destined to be sold to the consumer." It is interesting to note that this statement of Smith is quoted by T. H. Tooke in support of the doctrines of the banking-school. Cf. *An Inquiry into the Currency Principle*, London, 1844, p. 11.

instead, consider an economy in which the different stages and branches of production are divided into different independent enterprises. We can return later to the special case of single-enterprise production considered by Messrs. Foster and Catchings. But we will adhere throughout to another assumption which they make : the assumption that the amount of money in circulation remains unchanged. It is especially important to do this because most of the criticisms of the theory which have been made up to the present have sought the solution of the alleged dilemma chiefly in a proportional adjustment of the supply of money to the enlarged volume of production.[1] To me, at any rate, the fundamental error of the theory seems to arise rather in the presentation of the origin of the dilemma, the supply of money remaining unchanged. I shall return to the question of the effects of a change in the supply of money in the last section, in which I deal with Messrs. Foster and Catchings' proposals for positive reform.

What happens, then, under the conditions assumed, when somebody saves a part of his income hitherto devoted to consumption, or when a company does not distribute its profits, and the sums thus saved are reinvested in production ? At first, clearly the demand which is directed to means of production increases, and that directed to consumption goods correspondingly

[1] Cf. the criticism of F. L. Olmsted (op. cit., p. 68), where it is expressly stated : " This brings us back to the ' Dilemma,' and also brings us back to *the obvious and only escape from the Dilemma ;* namely, the progressive increase, in relation to the price-level of goods, of the scale of money compensation to individuals for their productive effort if that productive effort is progressively increasing in efficiency." (Italics mine.)

decreases. Does that mean that the expenditure on production will now be greater than is justified by the sums of money which will be available for the purchase of consumption goods ?

That this need not be the case is surely clear from the most superficial consideration of the modern capitalistic economy. For at every moment of time raw materials, semi-finished products, and other means of production are coming into the market, the value of which is several times greater than the value of the consumption goods which are simultaneously offered in the market for consumption goods.[1] It follows that the sum spent on the purchase of means of production of all kinds at any period is several times greater than the sum spent on the purchase of consumption goods at the same time. The fact that the total costs of production are, nevertheless, not greater than the value of the consumption goods produced is explained by the circumstance that every good on its way from raw material to finished product is exchanged against money as many times, on the average, as the amount of money expended on the purchase of means of production at every period exceeds the amount spent on consumption goods. And it is just a lengthening of this average process of production (which, *on our assumption*, shows itself in an increase of the number of independent stages of production) which makes it possible, when new

[1] M. W. Holtrop computes on the basis of statistical data taken from publications of I. Fisher and the National Bureau of Economic Research that in the United States in the year 1912 the sum of all money payments was more than twelve times larger than the sum of all money incomes (*De omloopssnelheid van het geld*, Amsterdam, 1928, p. 181). Cf. also his further exposition which gives interesting figures in regard to the variations of this proportion in the course of the trade cycle.

savings are available, to produce a greater amount of consumption goods from the same amount of original means of production.

The proposition that savings can only bring about an increase in the volume of production by permitting a greater and more productive " roundaboutness " in the methods of production has been demonstrated so fully by the classical analysis of Böhm-Bawerk that it does not require further examination. It is necessary here only to go further into certain monetary aspects of the phenomenon.

The questions which interest us are as follows : how does the increase in the money stream *available for productive purposes* following the investment of new savings distribute the additional demand for means of production through the economic system, and under what conditions is this distribution effected in such a way as to achieve the purpose of saving with the smallest possible disturbance. After what has been said already in this connection it will be of fundamental importance to distinguish between changes in the demand for original means of production, *i.e.*, labour and land, and changes in the demand for means of production which are themselves products (intermediate products or capital goods) such as semi-finished goods, machinery, implements, etc. On the other hand it is not important for our present purpose to distinguish between durable and non-durable means of production because it is irrelevant, for instance, that a loom has only to be renewed after eight periods of time, since, in a continuous process of production, this amounts to the same thing as if every eighth loom has to be renewed in every period.

For the sake of simplicity, we may assume that the path from the original means of production to the final product is of equal length for all parts of the total money stream, although, in fact, this differs according to the moment when the particular original means of production are employed in the different stages of production ; so that the assumed uniform length of the roundabout ways of production only corresponds to the *average* length of the various processes which lead to the production of a consumption good. The only case in real life strictly corresponding to this assumption would be the production of a good requiring expenditure of labour only at the beginning of the production process, the rest being left to nature ; as, for example, in the case of the planting of a tree. But even this would only completely conform to our assumption if the saplings changed hands every year, *i.e.*, if one man held one-year saplings, another two-year saplings, and so on. This difficulty only arises because, for purposes of exposition, it is easier to treat the average length of production as if it were uniform for all processes. In the real world, of course, it is the very fact that the period between the expenditure of the original means of production and the completion of the consumers' goods is different for every original means of production used, which makes it necessary that the goods should pass through several hands before they are ready for consumption. We assume, therefore, that, for example, the value of all means of production coming to the market during one period is eight times as great as the value of the consumption goods produced during the same period, and the latter is sold for 1,000 units of money, say pounds sterling. We disregard the differences in value conditioned by interest, that is to say, we make the assumption that interest on capital employed, together with the remuneration of the original means of production, is paid out only in the highest stage of production. The whole process of production and the circulation of money connected with it can then be represented schematically in the following way :

SCHEME A[1]

Demand for consumption goods (=products of stage of production No. 1)		£ 1,000

Demand for the products of the stages of production	No. 2	..	1,000
	No. 3	..	1,000
	No. 4	..	1,000
	No. 5	..	1,000
	No. 6	..	1,000
	No. 7	..	1,000
	No. 8	..	1,000
	No. 9	..	1,000

Total demand for produced means of production—8 × 1,000 =	.. 8,000

Relation of the demand for consumption goods to the demand for produced means of production—1 : 8.

Such a table represents at once both the products of the various stages of production coming on to the market *simultaneously* with the consumption goods

[1] If it were desired, in order to bring the scheme closer to reality to demonstrate, instead of the average length of the production process, the various lengths of its particular branches, it should be represented somewhat as follows :

and the *successive* intermediary products from which the actual product finally emerges, since, in a stationary economy, these are the same. We exhibit, that is to say, the total supply of goods originating in one branch of production (or, if the scheme is applied to the whole economy, all branches of production), and coming on to the market in one period of time. The sums paid at the ninth stage of production for the original means of production correspond necessarily with the value of the consumption goods, and form the origin of the funds for which the consumption goods are sold.

Let us assume, then, that the owners of the original means of production spend from their total income of

			£		£
Demand for consumption goods (=products of stage of production	No. 1)	...	1,000		58.8
	No. 2	...	941.2		58.8
	No. 3	...	882.4		58.8
	No. 4	...	823.5		58.8
	No. 5	...	764.8		58.8
	No. 6	...	705.9		58.8
	No. 7	...	647.6	From which	58.8
	No. 8	...	588.2	we have to	58.8
Demand for products of the	No. 9	...	529.4	deduct for	58.8
stages of production	No. 10	...	470.6	original	58.8
	No. 11	...	411.8	means of	58.8
	No. 12	...	352.9	production	58.8
	No. 13	...	294.1		58.8
	No. 14	...	235.3		58.8
	No. 15	...	176.5		58.8
	No. 16	...	117.6		58.8
	No. 17	...	58.8		58.8

Total demand for produced means of production ... 8,000.0

Total demand for original means of production 1,000.0

Relation of the demand for consumption goods to the demand for produced means of production—1 : 8.

Such an exposition, more complete than the former, alters nothing of its results, but complicates considerably the clarity of the presentation.

£1,000 only £900, and invest in production the remaining £100 thus saved.   There is, therefore, £8,100 now available for the purchase of production goods, and the relation between the demand for consumption goods and the demand for production goods changes from 1 : 8 to 1 : 9.

In order that the increased sum of money now available for the purchase of means of production should be profitably utilised, the average number of stages of production must increase from eight to nine ; the situation, represented in Scheme A, has therefore to be altered in the following way :

SCHEME B

(£100 is saved and invested)

	£
Demand for consumption goods (=products of stage of production No. 1) ..	900

		£
Demand for the products of the stages of	No. 2 ..	900
	No. 3 ..	900
	No. 4 ..	900
	No. 5 ..	900
Demand for the products of the stages of production	No. 6 ..	900
	No. 7 ..	900
	No. 8 ..	900
	No. 9 ..	900
	No. 10 ..	900

Total demand for produced means of production—9 × 900 =   .. 8,100

Relation of the demand for consumption goods to the demand for produced means of production—1 : 9.

In this case also, the total sum which is spent in the last stage for the original means of production, and which is therefore available as income for the purchase of the product coincides with the value of the product after the necessary adjustments have taken place. The allocation of the additional means of production has been effected by maintaining the equilibrium between costs of production and the prices of consumption goods in such a way that the money stream has been lengthened and narrowed down correspondingly, *i.e.*, the average number of the successive turnovers during the productive process has risen in the same ratio as the demand for means of production in relation to the demand for consumption goods has increased. If the supply of money remains unaltered this is necessarily connected with a fall in the prices of the factors of production, the unchanged amount of which (disregarding the increase of capital) has to be exchanged for £900 ; and a *still greater fall* in the prices of consumption goods, the volume of which has increased on account of the utilisation of more roundabout methods of production while their total money value has diminished from £1,000 to £900.

This demonstrates at any rate the *possibility* that, by an increase in the money stream going to production and a diminution of that going to consumption, production *can* still be organised in such a way that the products can be sold at remunerative prices. It remains to show (1) that with an unchanged amount of money, production will be governed by prices so that such an adjustment does take place, (2) that by such an adjustment of production the purpose of saving is achieved in the most favourable way, and (3) that on the other hand every change in the volume of currency, especially every monetary policy aiming at the stability of the prices of consumption goods (or any other prices) renders the adaptation of production to the new supply of saving more difficult and indeed frustrates more or less the end of saving itself.

VIII

In order to remain as faithful as possible to the example which Messrs. Foster and Catchings have put in the foreground, let us consider the case of a joint stock company reinvesting a portion of its profits which was hitherto distributed. In what way will it utilise the additional capital ? This utilisation may be different in different individual cases, yet important conclusions may be drawn from a consideration of the general possibilities of additional investments.

In principle it is possible for a single enterprise—in contrast to the whole industry—to utilise the available amount of capital for extending production by retaining existing methods but employing larger quantities of *all* factors.[1] We can leave the possibility of this out of

[1] In practice, such a *linear* extension of production will be of importance in so far as, by an increase in the supply of capital, not only will the share of capital in every branch of production increase, but there will be an increase in the relative size of more capitalistic branches of production as compared with less capitalistic ones, *i.e.*, the former will employ *more* labour, and this extension of the whole undertaking can so far overshadow the increase in the relative share of capital as to create the impression of a linear (proportional) extension of the more capitalistic undertakings. Even if the proportion between capital and the original means of production employed remains absolutely constant in the individual industries, but the more capitalistic undertakings were extended at the expense of the less capitalistic ones (as may be the case with

consideration for the moment, as our undertaking could only get additional labour and other original means of production by drawing them away from other undertakings, by outbidding them. And this process will change the relative proportion of capital to the other factors in the other enterprise, and thus a transition of production to new methods will become necessary. This is clearly the general economic effect of the increase of capital, and it is this in which we are interested. For the sake of simplicity let us assume, then, that the transition has already taken place in the first enterprise which undertook the savings.

But if a " linear " extension of production is ruled out, and the undertaking has to utilise its relative increase in capital supply for a transition to more capitalistic methods, there remain two main types of investment for the additional capital which have to be considered. These are usually distinguished as investment in fixed capital or durable producers' goods, and in circulating capital or non-durable producers' goods respectively. Up to now in following Messrs. Foster and Catchings we have only considered investment in circulating capital, in future we shall have to distinguish between these two possibilities.

Whether in any given case investment in fixed capital or in circulating capital is the more profitable, and is therefore undertaken, depends on the technical conditions of the concrete case, and therefore cannot

undertakings of average roundaboutness), this implies, from the point of view of the whole industry, a transition to more capitalistic methods. (It may perhaps be mentioned here that the original German terms which the translator has rendered as " roundaboutness " and more or less " capitalistic " were " *Kapitalintensität* " and " *kapitalintensiv.*")

be decided *a priori*. For analytical purposes it is desirable to treat these two cases separately, both as regards the conditions which must be given in order to render more capitalistic methods profitable, and also as regards the effect on prices.

IX

As regards investment in *fixed capital* (*i.e.*, durable means of production), the case is relatively simple. Messrs. Foster and Catchings leave this case entirely out of account (a fact on which, as we have already mentioned, Mr. A. B. Adams bases his criticism) and Mr. P. W. Martin applies a similar theory of his own expressly to the case of investment in circulating capital only.[1] What we shall have to say here, therefore, will hardly meet with much opposition, and for this reason it will be easier in this connection to develop the analysis which is relevant also for the subsequent investigation.

In order that new investment in fixed capital may be profitable, it is necessary that the increase in receipts from the increased product following the investment should be sufficient to cover the interest and depreciation of the invested capital. The rate of interest must be somewhat higher where the new investments are made than in the alternative employments which are open to them, but somewhat lower than the rate of interest paid hitherto. It is just the circumstance that the rate of interest has fallen and that the investment in question is the nearest in the scale of profitableness

---

[1] Cf. *Unemployment and Purchasing Power*, p. 15.

which determines that it, and no other, shall be undertaken. In judging its profitableness, account must be taken of the fact that the enlarged product following the new investment can only be sold in the long run at prices lower relatively to the prices of original means of production than hitherto. This is partly because, owing to the co-operation of new capital, more consumption goods will be produced from a given quantity of original means of production ; and also because a greater amount of consumption goods must be sold against the income of the original means of production and of capital, and the increase in the income from the latter (if it occurs at all—if the increase in capital is not more than compensated by the fall in the interest rate) must always be relatively less than the increase of consumption goods.[1]

If the quantity of money remains unchanged, the unavoidable fall in the relative prices of consumption goods will also manifest itself absolutely. It is in this way that the relative fall will establish itself at the moment when the new consumption goods come on to the market. If the supply of money is kept constant, this effect of every extension of production will be well known to producers and they will therefore *only choose such employments for the investment of new savings as remain profitable even if prices are expected to fall.* But these employments—and this, as we shall see presently,

---

[1] The fall in the rate of interest necessitates *ipso facto* such a relative change in the prices of means of production and of products because, in a state of equilibrium, the rate of interest must exactly correspond with the difference between the two. With regard to the relation between changes in the rate of interest and changes in relative prices, cf. the appendix to my essay " Das intertemporale Gleichgewichtssystem der Preise und die Bewegungen des Geldwertes," *Weltwirtschaftliches Archiv*, Vol. XXVIII, July, 1928.

is the essential point—are the only ones through which the social advantages of saving can be realised without loss.

Even if the volume of money is increased so that the prices of consumption goods do not fall, a new equilibrium must inevitably be established between costs of production and the prices of products. This can come about—if a fall in the prices of consumption goods is excluded—in two ways : either by a rise in the prices of means of production ; or by a return to the previous, shorter, less productive method of production ; or by both of these ways together. What actually happens depends on where and when the additional money is injected into the economic system. If the increase in the supply of money were only to take place at the time when the additional volume of consumption goods comes on to the market and in such a way as to render it directly available for the purchase of consumption goods,[1] the expectation of unchanged prices for products would result in a portion of the additional amount, rendered available for the purchase of means of production through saving, not being utilised for a lengthening of the production process, *i.e.*, the formation of new capital ; it would simply serve to drive up the prices of the means of production. Because of the expectation of stable prices for the products, *more* openings for the new savings will appear profitable than can actually be exploited with their aid. The rate of interest is only sufficient to limit alternatives to those most profitable when price-relations are also in

[1] This is the suggestion made by Messrs. Foster and Catchings ; we shall have occasion to go into this case more extensively in the last section, when we come to criticise their proposals for reform.

equilibrium with it. Competitive selection must therefore take place in the market for the means of
production, *i.e.*, the prices of means of production must
rise until only so many extensions of the productive
process appear profitable at those prices as can actually
be carried out by the new savings. That simply means
that a portion of the savings will not be utilised for the
creation of capital, but merely for the purpose of
increasing the prices of available means of production.

But the assumption that the supply of money will
only be increased when the enlarged volume of consumption goods comes on to the market has little
probability. In the first place, the fact that new
savings offer possibilities for the extension of production
will, as a rule (according to the prevalent opinion,
quite justifiably), give rise to an increase in the volume
of money in the form of producers' credits. On the
other hand, the fact that, in spite of the more capitalistic
and more productive methods, the prices of the
products do not fall, will provide an incentive to take
up additional loans from the banks far beyond the sum
voluntarily saved, and will thus increase the demand
for means of production much more than would be
justified by the new savings. The rise in the prices of
these means of production conditioned by it, will
gradually cause the excessive price-margin between
these goods and consumption goods to disappear (and
thus take away the incentive for further extensions of
credit) ; at the same time, more means of production
than are justified by the new savings will be transferred
for use in longer processes (*i.e.*, more lengthy processes
will be undertaken than can be carried out). In other
words, it will be possible, through an increase in the

volume of money, to draw away as many factors from the consumption goods industries, over and above the quota voluntarily saved, as to enable at first the commencement of all enlargements of fixed capital which appear profitable at the lower rate of interest having regard to the unchanged prices.

All these investments, however, can be carried on only so long as the new money used for extensions of production is not utilised by the owners of the factors of production, to whom it is paid, for the purchase of consumption goods or so long as the increase in the demand for consumption goods is offset by a progressive increase in the supply of new productive credits.[1] As soon as the increase in the volume of credits granted to producers is no longer sufficient to take away as many means of production from the provision of current consumption as would be required for the execution of all the projects which appear profitable under the lower rate of interest and the unchanged price relationship between consumption goods and means of production, then the increasing utilisation of means of production for the provision of current needs through less lengthy processes of production will drive up the prices of means of production, both absolutely and relatively to consumption goods, and thus render unprofitable those extensions of production which only became possible through the policy of price stabilisation.

As, in the case under consideration, we are dealing with extensions of durable plant, which as a rule must be left in their previous employments even if they

---

[1] Cf. my *Monetary Theory and the Trade Cycle*, 1933.

become unprofitable (even if their quasi-rents fall to such a level as to drive their value much below the cost of production, and thus prevent their replacement) the adjustments necessary will only proceed very slowly and with great sacrifices of capital. But, apart from this loss of a portion of the savings, the final equilibrium of production will establish itself in that position where it would have been established right from the beginning had no increase in money supply intervened ; that is to say, at that point where the diminution in the cost per unit of product brought about by the investment is just great enough to sell the larger quantity of the final product despite the fact that, owing to savings, only a smaller proportion of the total money stream goes to purchase it than hitherto. Although the schematic representation given above is only completely applicable to the case (to which we shall return later) of investment in circulating capital, it is also true in the case of investment in fixed capital that the necessary fall in the price of the final product manifests itself not only in a fall of the price per unit (which must take place even if an unchanged money stream goes to buy a larger product) but also in a diminution in the proportion of the total money stream which is available for the purchase of consumption goods.

The difference between this case and that of investment in circulating capital lies in the fact that in the former case the demand for means of production in relation to the demand for consumption goods does not, in the long run, increase by the whole of the newly-invested sum, but only by the amount necessary to keep the additional capital intact. So long as the production of additional capital is going on, the demand for consumption goods diminishes by the whole of the amount newly saved and invested.[1] The transference of factors of production for the production of new means of production which is conditioned by this diminution, is, however, partly temporary. As soon as the new durable means of production are ready, and the production of final products can be correspondingly increased with their aid, the sums available for their purchase in the hands of consumers are not diminished by the value of the newly-invested capital, but only by that amount which is necessary for their upkeep and amortisation. But an amount of this magnitude will always have to be put aside by the entrepreneur, and thus withdrawn from consumption.

Even if he can only proceed to a renewal of fixed capital (in the absence of new savings) when the old is fully amortised, the sums accumulating for amortisation will increase the current demand for means of production in the meantime for the purpose of producing new means of production. The entrepreneur must try to invest these sums to the best advantage until he needs them himself, and thus will increase the supply of capital and exercise a further pressure on interest rates. Without going into the complicated processes which are conditioned by the temporary accommodation of sums accumulated for amortisation, it may be said that they signify a temporary transformation of capital (mostly in

[1] In order to avoid too much complication in the exposition I disregard the case of an increase in the supply of capital leading to a more than proportional increase in the supply of fixed capital (or vice versa) which may occur owing to the fact that a fall in the rate of interest may render it profitable to transform already existing investments in circulating capital into fixed capital.

circulating form), but they also form a current demand for the production of capital goods. As a result, an increase in fixed capital will have the same effects as if every single undertaking continuously renewed the wear and tear of its plant, *i.e.*, spent uniformly a greater proportion of its receipts than before the investment in new capital on the purchase of intermediate products, and a smaller proportion on the purchase of original means of production. As this implies a corresponding diminution in the amounts available for the purchase of consumption goods, investment in fixed capital will therefore also have the effect of " stretching " the money stream, that is to say, it becomes longer and narrower ; or, in the terminology of Messrs. Foster and Catchings, the circuit velocity of money diminishes.

x

The same effects manifest themselves still more directly in the case of an investment of new savings in *circulating capital*. And yet, as the examples of Messrs. Foster and Catchings, Mr. P. W. Martin, and Mr. A. B. Adams show, this necessary concomitant phenomenon of *every* increase of capital, is, in just this case, very easily overlooked. The explanation lies in the fact that the case of a single enterprise, which can always utilise its increased circulating capital for a proportional increase of its labourers and other means of production, is applied directly to the economic system as a whole, although it should be clear that an increase in capital, whether fixed or circulating, can only show itself in the economic system as a whole in an increase in intermediate products in relation to original means of production.

One of the most frequent cases of an increase in circulating capital—it is the case which led Messrs. Foster and Catchings and their adherents to overlook completely the capital function of the invested savings —is the case which has already been mentioned[1] of a relative extension of the more capitalistic branches of production at the expense of the less capitalistic ones. In this case, original means of production will be taken away from the latter and utilised in the former, without an increase in their fixed capital, so that at first the original means of production employed there increase relatively to the fixed capital. As has already been emphasised, it is not the increase in the volume of original means of production employed which is significant here, but the fact that they are now employed in a way which causes, on the average, a longer period of time to elapse between their employment and the emergence of their final product, and therefore more intermediary products to exist at any moment than before. It is just because an increase in the supply of capital enables relatively more roundabout processes to be undertaken that the more capitalistic undertakings can now employ more labour (and possibly more land).

At first the increased capital supply will result in the more capitalistic undertakings demanding more original means of production than hitherto, acquiring these by overbidding other undertakings. As more units of factors can only be acquired at a higher cost per unit, the extent to which they are able to do so depends on

[1] See p. 229, note 1.

their expectations of an increase in total receipts from an increase in the volume of the product.   In no case, however, will they be able to spend the total amount of new capital on increased employment of original means of production. Even to the extent that capital *is* used for that purpose in a single enterprise, this does not imply that part of the new capital is definitely used to remunerate original means of production. By exactly the same amount by which this enterprise increases its expenditure on original means of production because it expects a corresponding increase of its receipts, other enterprises will have to cut down expenditure on original means of production because their receipts will have undergone a corresponding decrease, and will be able to invest that part as capital.

On the assumption, which we still adhere to, that the products of every stage of production come on to the market and are acquired there by the entrepreneur of the next stage, it is evident that only a portion of the newly-invested savings can be spent on original means of production, while another and, in the modern, highly developed, economy, much greater portion must be used to acquire additional quantities of the products of the previous stage of production. This portion will be all the larger, the greater the number of the stages of production (represented by independent enterprises) and, as a rule, several times as large as the portion spent on wages, etc.[1] It serves the purpose of providing all the stages

---

[1] While, in assuming only one stage of production, the value of all products at the end of the production process equals the value of the means of production employed ; on the other hand, on the assumption that equal quantities of original means of production are employed at every stage (the case represented in the footnote at

of production (up to the last stage, where the final products of the original means of production now employed in the longer processes emerge) with a correspondingly larger amount of intermediate products ; or, which means the same thing, it makes it possible for the additional original means of production to be paid for continuously, period by period, so long as their additional product has not yet reached the final stage.

After what we have seen in the case of investment in fixed capital, we can formulate the problem before us by asking how, when new investment in circulating capital takes place, the price-relations between production goods and consumption goods must adjust themselves in order that production shall be extended to such and only to such an extent that the new savings just suffice to carry out the enlarged processes ?

Again we can start by assuming that, in the long run, the new capital investment must bring about a fall of the price of the products in relation to the prices of the means of production. If entrepreneurs expect—as, if the volume of money were kept constant, they ought to expect from experience—that the prices of the products will fall absolutely, then from the outset they will only extend production in such proportions as to ensure profitableness even if the relative prices of products (as opposed to the means of production) fall. This means that the increase in production will be limited, right from the beginning, to that extent which

p. 229 above) the value of the latter is one and one-half times as great if two, two and one-half times if four, and five and one-half times if ten stages of production are assumed, and so on. (Cf. Böhm-Bawerk, *Positive Theory*, 4th German Ed., Vol. I, p. 397.)

can permanently be maintained. If, however, unchanged prices are expected for the products, it would seem profitable at first to attempt a further extension of production ; and that to the extent which would seem profitable at the present prices of the means of production. The latter will not increase at first by as much as will finally be necessary for the establishment of equilibrium ; they will rise only gradually as the increased demand for original means of production is passed on from the higher to the lower stages. With the progressive increase in the prices of the means of production, not only that portion of the additional production which would not have been undertaken if falling prices had been expected will become unprofitable ; but also—since hitherto too many means of production were used up, a greater scarcity ensues, and their prices will increase more than they otherwise would—some part of the production which would have been profitable but for the dissipation of a part of the supply of means of production. Every attempt to prevent the fall of prices by increasing the volume of money will have the effect of increasing production to an extent that it is impossible to maintain, and thus part of the savings will be wasted.

XI

Let us now consider the case—fundamental to Messrs. Foster and Catchings' analysis—in which production is completely integrated vertically, the case in which all stages of one branch of production are united in one undertaking. In such circumstances there is no

necessity to utilise certain parts of the money stream
for the purchase of intermediate products ; only
consumption goods proper on the one hand, and the
original means of production on the other are exchanged
against money. The examination of this case is essential
to prove the validity of our thesis—partly because, in
the existing economic order, the various stages of production are not always divided into separate undertakings, and therefore an increase in the number of
stages need not necessarily bring about an increase in
the number of *independent undertakings*, but chiefly
because the lengthening of the production process
need not manifest itself in an increase in the number
of *distinguishable stages* (as for the sake of clarity of
exposition we have assumed up to the present), but
simply in the lengthening of a continuous production
process.

It is, however, impossible for reasons which are
obvious, but which were overlooked by their critics, to
follow Messrs. Foster and Catchings in their assumption
that all the *various branches* of production are also
united in a single enterprise. If that were so, there
would be no inducement for that undertaking to save
money, or to take up the money savings of private
individuals ; and there would thus be no opportunity
for private individuals to invest their savings. If that
undertaking is the only one of its kind, and therefore
the only one using original means of production, it can—
just as the dictator of a Socialist economy can—
determine at will what proportion of the original
means of production shall go for the satisfaction of
current consumption, and what proportion to the
making or renewal of means of production. Only if,

and in so far as, there is competition between the various branches of production for the supply of means of production, is it necessary, in order to obtain the additional means of production requisite for an enlargement of capital equipment, to have the disposal of additional amounts of money (either saved for that purpose or newly created). Only in such circumstances does there exist, accordingly, any inducement to save.

As it is clearly inadmissible to start from an assumption which renders the phenomenon to be investigated (*i.e.*, the saving of individuals and companies) totally meaningless,[1] we can go no further in our investigations than the case of the complete vertical integration of single branches of production. But here, after what has been demonstrated above, it can be shown without difficulty that, if a transformation of money savings into additional real capital is to come about, the investment must lead to a diminution in the money stream available for the purchase of consumption goods[2] (*i.e.*, to that slowing down of the " circuit velocity of money " of which Messrs. Foster and Catchings are so afraid), and that savings can only be utilised to the best advantage when the supply of money remains unaltered and the price per unit of the enlarged volume of goods diminishes.

Let us assume, therefore, that such an undertaking comprising all stages of production in one branch

---

[1] Messrs. Foster and Catchings, it is true, expressly declare that their assumption about the number of undertakings is insignificant and in no way invalidates their reasoning (*Profits*, p. 270). They do not put forward any proof, however, and the fact that, even in trying to justify it, they do not realise that savings would be entirely meaningless under these circumstances, is the best proof of how completely they misunderstand the real function of saving.

[2] At any rate for so long as the transition of production goes on.

extends its production by " corporate saving " so that during the extension of capital equipment the sums necessary for this purpose are raised from profits (*i.e.*, interest on capital and earnings of management). In this way it will be able to keep its demand for original means of production constant, although, owing to the transformation of production, it can temporarily only bring a smaller volume of ready consumption goods on to the market, and its current receipts must fall. It is a necessary condition of the longer duration of the new production process that either the undertaking cannot for a short period bring any goods on to the market, or if it apportions its sales uniformly through time, it can offer only a smaller amount of the finished product for a longer period. The savings accumulated through individual profits serve just this very purpose of making good the diminution of receipts and enabling it to undertake the more productive, but more lengthy process. It must not, therefore, devote the whole sum to obtain more original means of production than before, for part must be used for bridging over the time during which its receipts will fall below current expenditure. The time during which it will be able to cover the difference between outgoings and receipts by saving forms the limit to the possible lengthening of the production process.

As long as the new investment is going on, a larger sum of money will be expended on means of production than that which is received from the sale of consumption goods at the same time. That occurs, as Messrs. Foster and Catchings repeatedly and correctly emphasise, by " money that is once used to bring about the production of goods being again used to bring about the production of goods before it is used to bring about the consumption of goods," *i.e.*, that sums which represent the remuneration of capital and entrepreneurial services are utilised for the purchase of means of production instead of the purchase of consumption goods. What Messrs. Foster and Catchings misunderstand is the function of and the necessity for this relative increase in the demand for production goods and the corresponding diminution in the sales of consumption goods. It is the natural and necessary corollary of saving, which, in terms of Crusoe-economics, consists in the fact that less consumption goods are produced and consumed than could be produced from the means of production employed. The simultaneous increase in the demand for original means of production, *i.e.*, the increase in the sums spent in the last stage of production (from which the original factors are remunerated) during one economic period, does not imply that at a later stage the money demand for consumption goods has to be increased by a similar amount in order to facilitate the sale of the enlarged volume of finished goods. The increase in the demand for means of production originates from the *lengthening* of the production process ; so long as this is going on, more means of production are produced at every stage than are consumed at the next ; production will serve the double purpose of satisfying current demand with the older (and shorter) process, and future demand with the new (longer) process. The demand for means of production is therefore, so long as new saving is going on, greater in relation to the demand for consumption goods than in the absence of savings because (in contrast to the stationary economy where the product

of the means of production used in every period equals
the goods consumed in that period) *the product of the
means of production applied during the saving period
will be consumed during a period which is longer than
the saving period itself.*[1]

In order that the means saved should really bring
about that extension of productive equipment for
which they are just sufficient, the expected prices
must make just that extension seem profitable. But
that is (as should be clear by now, without a repetition
of what has been said before) only the case when the
money available for the purchase of the larger product
is not greater than the part of the current outlays
which served for *its* production. And since longer
processes are more productive, in order that this may
be the case, the unit prices of the product must now
be less. Every expectation of future receipts greater
than those necessary to cover the smaller costs per
unit will lead to such excessive extensions of production
as will become unprofitable as soon as the relative
prices are no longer disturbed by the injection of new
money.

XII

There is no danger, therefore, that too much money
will be spent on production in relation to the sums
available for consumption so long as the relative

---

[1] That is correctly recognised by Mr. A. B. Adams in his criticism
mentioned above of Messrs. Foster and Catchings in *Profits,
Progress and Prosperity*, where it is expressly stated (p. 18) : " If
the physical volume of current output of consumers' goods should
equal the physical volume of all goods produced currently there could
be no accumulation of permanent capital—there could be no real
savings."

diminution in the demand for consumption goods is of a permanent nature and the latter does not, as *must* be the case with changes in the relative demand brought about by changes in the volume of money, increase again and drive the prices of the original means of production to such a height that the completion of the more capitalistic processes becomes unprofitable. As it is not the absolute level of the prices of the product, but only their relative level in comparison with factor prices which determines the remunerativeness of production, it is, therefore, never the absolute size of the demand for consumption goods, but the relative size of the demands for the means of production to be used for the various methods of producing consumption goods that determines this relative profitableness. *In principle, therefore, any portion, however small, of the total money stream ought to be sufficient to take up the consumption goods produced with the aid of the other portions, as long as, for any reason, the demand for consumption goods does not rise suddenly in relation to the demand for means of production, in which case the disproportionate amount of intermediate products (disproportionate in relation to the new distribution of demand) can no longer be sold at prices which cover costs.*

The problem is therefore not the absolute amount of money spent for consumption goods, but only the question whether the relative demand for the consumption goods is not *greater* in relation to the money stream utilised for productive purposes than the current flow of consumption goods in relation to the simultaneous output of means of production. In this, and only in this case, will a disproportionate supply of means of production, and thus the impossibility of remunerative employment, arise, *not because the demand for consumption goods is too small, but on the contrary because it is too large and too urgent* to render the execution of lengthy roundabout processes profitable. The idea of a general over-production in relation to the money *incomes* of the consumers as Messrs. Foster and Catchings conceive it, is as untenable in a money economy as under barter. A crisis occurs only when the available supply of intermediate products in all stages of production in relation to the supply of consumers' goods is greater than the demand for the former in relation to the demand for the latter. Apart from the case of spontaneous consumption of capital, this can only arise when either the *supply* of means of production, or the *demand* for consumption goods has been artificially and temporarily extended by credit policy. In either case a price relation will arise between means of production and finished products which renders production unprofitable.

XIII

That concludes our criticism of the cases in which savings are supposed to involve trade depression if the supply of money is not increased. The whole question is very similar to the old problem whether, when productivity is increasing, prices should remain stable or fall. As Mr. A. H. Hansen has pointed out, the argument of Messrs. Foster and Catchings is applicable not only to the effect of saving but also to all other cases of increasing productivity.[1] To this extent, both authors became the victims of that uncritical fear of

[1] *Business Cycle Theory*, p. 44.

any kind of fall in prices which is so widespread to-day, and which lends a cloak to all the more refined forms of inflationism—a fashion which is all the more regrettable since many of the best economists, A. Marshall, [1] N. G. Pierson, [2] W. Lexis, [3] F. Y. Edgeworth, [4] Professor Taussig [5] in the past, and more recently Professor Mises, [6] Dr. Haberler, [7] Professor Pigou, [8] and Mr. D. H. Robertson, [9] have repeatedly emphasised the misconception underlying it.

But in the special case which Messrs. Foster and Catchings have made the basis of their proposals for stabilisation, their argument is based on a different and less excusable misconception. What they entirely lack is any understanding of the function of capital and interest. The gap in their analytical equipment in this respect goes so far that, in their exposition of the theory of price, while most of the general problems are very thoroughly and adequately treated, any examination of this question is utterly lacking, and in the

---

[1] Cf. his evidence before the Gold and Silver Commission of 1887, now reprinted in *Official Papers by Alfred Marshall*, London, 1926, especially p. 91.

[2] Cf., *e.g.*, *Gold Scarcity* (translated into German by R. Reisch) in the *Zeitschrift für Volkswirtschaft, Sozialpolitik und Verwaltung*, Vol. IV, No. 1, Vienna, 1895, especially p. 23.

[3] On several occasions in connection with the bimetallist question, *e.g.*, in the *Verhandlungen der deutschen Silberkomission*, Berlin, 1894. Similarly C. Helfferich, E. Nasse, and L. Bamberger.

[4] Cf. "Thoughts on Monetary Reform," *Economic Journal*, 1895, reprinted under "Questions connected with Bimetallism" in *Papers Relating to Political Economy*, Vol. I, p. 421.

[5] Cf. *The Silver Situation in the United States*, New York, 1893, pp. 104–12.

[6] Cf. *Geldwertsstabilisierung und Konjunkturpolitik*, Jena, 1928, p. 30.

[7] Cf. *Der Sinn der Indexzahlen*, Tübingen, 1927, pp. 112 *et seq.*

[8] Cf. *Industrial Fluctuations*, 2nd Ed., London, 1929, pp. 182 *et seq.* and 255 *et seq.*

[9] Cf. *Money*, 2nd Ed., London, 1928.

alphabetical index of *Profits* " capital " is only mentioned as a source of income. I cannot help feeling that, if they had extended their investigations to this field, or even if they had merely thought it worth their while to make themselves familiar with the existing literature of a question so cogent to their problem, they would themselves have realised the untenable nature of their theory. In the literature of monetary theory (with the exception of the works of K. Wicksell and Professor Mises, which are probably inaccessible to them for linguistic reasons) they will, of course, look in vain for the necessary explanation, for so many writers on this subject still labour under the sway of the dogma of the necessity for a stable price-level, and this makes recognition of these interconnections extraordinarily difficult. But just as Mr. R. W. Souter, their prize-winning critic, recommended them to read Marshall, so I would recommend them, still more urgently, to make a thorough study of Böhm-Bawerk, whose main work, if only in the first edition, is available in English translation.

XIV

We have repeatedly had occasion while examining the theory of Messrs. Foster and Catchings to point to the effects which would ensue if the proposals based upon it were put into practice. But it may well be that the contrast between the real effects of such proposals and the expectations based upon them may not yet be sufficiently clear. And as similar demands are continually being brought forward everywhere for all kinds of reasons, it seems worth while finally attempting a systematic account of the actual consequences to be expected if they were really carried out.

It has already been explained that Messrs. Foster and Catchings' proposals for reform involve increasing the volume of money, either through consumers' credits or the financing of State expenditure, in order to bring about the sale at unchanged prices of a volume of products enlarged by an increase of saving. The effects of such increases of money spent on consumption can best be demonstrated by contrasting them with the effects of additional productive credits. We shall work under the assumption used in the previous analysis, where the different stages of production are in the hands of different undertakings. The application of this reasoning to that of the completely integrated branch of production should follow more or less of itself.

We may take as a starting-point the result of our previous demonstration of the effect of saving, the volume of money remaining unchanged (Scheme B, p. 231). According to this the relation of the demand for consumers' goods to the demand for means of production changed from £1,000 : £8,000 to £900 : £8,100, or from 1 : 8 to 1 : 9, so that the number of stages increased correspondingly from 9 to 10. Now let us assume that, in accordance with the proposal of Messrs. Foster and Catchings, at the moment when the enlarged product comes on to the market, the volume of money is increased by the same sum as the sums spent on production, i.e., by £100[1] and that this

[1] In fact we ought to take an increase of £200, since, as a consequence of saving, the difference between the sums spent on production and on consumption goods increases by that amount. As by taking this larger amount the effect demonstrated will only become more pronounced, it will suffice to regard the more simple case given in the text.

additional sum is spent exclusively on consumption
goods. Because of this, the demand for consumption
goods again increases from £900 to £1,000, while the
sums available for means of production remain
unchanged, so that the relation between the demand for
the two groups of goods changes from £900 : £8,100 to
£1,000 : £8,100, *i.e.*, the relative size of the demand for
means of production in comparison with the demand
for consumption goods falls from 9 times to 8.1 times
the latter. The transformation of production conditioned by this, in the form of a shortening of the
productive process, comes about in the manner represented in Scheme C. As the number of stages of production, under our assumption, must then be 8.1, the
last stage (No. 10) must be represented by a value
which is only one-tenth of the rest.

SCHEME C
(£100 is added to the circulation as credit to consumers.)

		£
Demand for consumption goods (= products of stage of production No. 1) ..		1,000

		£
	No. 2 ..	1,000
	No. 3 ..	1,000
	No. 4 ..	1,000
	No. 5 ..	1,000
Demand for the products of the stages of production	No. 6 ..	1,000
	No. 7 ..	1,000
	No. 8 ..	1,000
	No. 9 ..	1,000
	No. 10 ..	100

Total demand for produced means of
        production—8.1 × 1,000 =   .. 8,100

Demand for consumption goods in relation to the demand for produced means of production—1 : 8.1.

But this shortening of the production process to the point where it stood before the investment of new savings (cf. Scheme A, p. 230) need not be the final effect, if the increase in money occurs only once and is not repeated again and again. The extension of production became possible because producers consumed, instead of one-ninth (Scheme A), only one-tenth (Scheme B) of their total receipts, and utilised the rest for the purpose of keeping their capital intact. In so far as they persist in their endeavour to keep their capital intact, in spite of the diminution of the purchasing power of those parts of their receipts which are conditioned by the appearance of new money, the demand for consumption goods in relation to that for means of production will again shift in favour of the latter as soon as the demand for the former is no longer artificially extended through additional spending power. To this extent the shortening of the production process and the devaluation of fixed plant connected with it will only be temporary ; but this is contingent upon a cessation of the flow of additional money. What is important, however, is that (even in an expanding economic system) *such an inflationist enlargement of the demand for consumption goods must, in itself, bring about at once similar phenomena of crisis to those which are necessarily brought about in consequence of an increase in productive credits, as soon as the latter cease to increase or their rate of flow diminishes.*[1] This will be best understood if we represent this case schematically also. We again take Scheme B (p. 231) as our starting-point, assuming that, in accordance with prevalent opinion, the extension of production is taken as a justification for an extension in money supply. This extension, however, takes the form of productive credits. For simplicity, we assume that the additional money injected in the form of productive credits amounts to £900, and, therefore, the relation between the demand for consumption goods and the demand for production goods alters, as compared with the case represented in Scheme B, from £900 : £8,100 to £900 : £9,000, or from 1 : 9 to 1 : 10.

The proportional increase in the demand for means of production as compared with the demand for consumption goods permits an extension of the production process as compared with the position in Scheme B, thus :

[1] It would be a mistake to argue against the representation of the effect of consumptive credits above by saying that the War-inflation was also brought about by additional expenditure on consumption, and yet did not lead to crisis, but, on the contrary, to a boom. The War-inflation could never have led to such an extension of production as it actually did had the additional credits only been given to undertakings in the form of proceeds for the sale of products, and not—whether in the form of pre-payments or directly in productive credits—placed at their disposal in advance for the purpose of extending production. One should visualise what would have happened had the increase in the demand for consumption goods always preceded the increase in the sums available for the purchase of means of production. And one would soon realise that this would only have rendered production of the present extent unprofitable, and would have led to a diminution of the productive apparatus in the form of a consumption of capital. During the War, this phenomenon was also rendered invisible through the appearance of specious profits following currency depreciation, which caused entrepreneurs to overlook that they were, in fact, consuming capital.

SCHEME D

(In the situation depicted in Scheme B £900 are added
as credits to producers, first stage.)

		£
Demand for consumption goods (=products of stage of production No. 1) ..		900

			£
	No. 2 ..		900
	No. 3 ..		900
	No. 4 ..		900
	No. 5 ..		900
Demand for the products of the	No. 6 ..		900
stages of production	No. 7 ..		900
	No. 8 ..		900
	No. 9 ..		900
	No. 10 ..		900
	No. 11 ..		900

		£
Total demand for produced means of production—10 × 900 =	..	9,000

Demand for consumption goods in relation to the
demand for produced means of production—1 : 10.

This lengthening of the productive process, however,
can continue only so long as the demand for means of
production is kept at the same relative level through
still further additions of producers' credits ; *i.e.*, so
long and so far as the durable production goods
produced on account of the temporary increase in the
demand for means of production suffice to carry on
production of this extent. As soon and in so far as
neither of these two assumptions remains true, all
consumers whose real income was diminished through
the competition of the increased demand for means

of production will attempt to bring their consumption
up again to the previous level, and to utilise a
corresponding portion of their money income for the
purchase of consumption goods. But that means
that the demand for consumption goods will increase
again to more than one-tenth of the total demand for
goods of every stage. Accordingly, only a smaller
proportion of the total money stream goes to buy
produced means of production, and the following
changes in the structure of production will occur :

SCHEME E

(Same as Scheme D, second stage.)

		£
Demand for consumption goods (=products of stage of production No. 1) ..		1,000

	No. 2	..	1,000
	No. 3	..	1,000
	No. 4	..	1,000
	No. 5	..	1,000
Demand for the products of the	No. 6	..	1,000
stages of production	No. 7	..	1,000
	No. 8	..	1,000
	No. 9	..	1,000
	No. 10	..	1,000

Total demand for produced means of
               production—9 × 1,000   =   .. 9,000

Demand for consumption goods in relation to the
demand for produced means of production—1 : 9.

Without any further change in the volume of money,
and only because the increase in the form of productive

262 PROFITS, INTEREST AND INVESTMENT

credits has ceased, the whole production process, and thus the length of the circuit velocity of money, tends again to contract to the old level. This contraction, which naturally involves the loss of those means of production which are adapted to the longer processes, and which is directly occasioned by the rise in the price of the means of production brought about by an increase in the demand for consumption goods, which renders the longer processes unprofitable, is a typical phenomenon of any crisis. As is easily seen, it is of the same nature as the effects of a relative increase in the demand for consumption goods brought about by consumers' credits.

It is just because with *every* increase in the volume of money, whether it is made available first for consumption or first for production, the relative size of the demand for those means of production which already exists or which has been directly enlarged by an increase in money must eventually contract in relation to the demand for consumption goods, that a more or less severe reaction will follow. This frantic game of now enlarging, now contracting the productive apparatus through increases in the volume of money injected, now on the production, now on the consumption side, is always going on under the present organisation of currency. Both effects follow each other uninterruptedly and thus an extension or contraction of the productive process is brought about, according to whether credit-creation for productive purposes is accelerated or retarded. So long as the volume of money in circulation is continually changing, we cannot get rid of industrial fluctuations. In particular, every monetary policy which aims at stabilising the value of money and involves, therefore, an increase of its supply with every increase of production, must bring about those very fluctuations which it is trying to prevent.

But least of all is it possible to bring about stability by that " financing of consumption " which Messrs. Foster and Catchings recommend, since there would be added to the contraction of the production process which automatically follows from increases of productive credits a still further contraction because of the consumptive credits, and thus crises would be rendered exceptionally severe.   Only if administered with extraordinary caution and superhuman ability could it, perhaps, be made to prevent crises : if the artificial increase in the demand for consumption goods brought about by those credits were made exactly to cancel the increase in the demand for means of production brought about by the investment of the current flow of savings, thus preserving constant the proportion between the two, this might happen. *But such a policy would effectively prevent any increase in capital equipment and completely frustrate any saving whatever.*[1]   There can be no question, therefore, that in the long run, even a policy of this sort would bring about grave disturbances and the disorganisation of the economic system as a whole.   So that, we may say, in conclusion, that the execution of Messrs. Foster and Catchings' proposals would not prevent, but considerably aggravate, crises ;   that is, it would punish every attempt at capital creation by a loss of a portion of the capital.   Carried through to its logical conclusion, it would effectively prevent every real capital accumulation.

[1] Cf. the remarks of A. B. Adams, quoted above, p. 251, note 51.

INDEX OF AUTHORS CITED

265

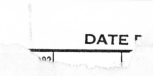

DATE [

092

M/